Here's what the critics say about Frommer's:

"Amazingly easy to use. Very portable, very complete."

—Booklist

"The only mainstream guide to list specific prices. The Walter Cronkite of guidebooks—with all that implies."

—Travel & Leisure

"Complete, concise, and filled with useful information."

—New York Daily News

"Hotel information is close to encyclopedic."
—Des Moines Sunday Register

"Detailed, accurate and easy-to-read information for all price ranges."

—Glamour Magazine

P O R T A B L E

Tampa &
St. Petersburg

2nd Edition

by Bill Goodwin

IDG Books Worldwide, Inc.
An International Data Group Company
Foster City, CA • Chicago, IL • Indianapolis, IN • New York, NY

ABOUT THE AUTHOR

Bill Goodwin began his career as an award-winning newspaper reporter before becoming legal counsel and speechwriter for two U.S. senators. He is also the author of *Frommer's Florida, Frommer's South Pacific,* and *Frommer's Virginia.*

IDG BOOKS WORLDWIDE, INC.

An International Data Group Company
919 E. Hillsdale Blvd.
Suite 400
Foster City, CA 94404

Find us online at **www.frommers.com**

ISBN 0-02-863795-X
ISSN 1044-2391

Editor: Naomi P. Kraus
Production Editor: Tammy Ahrens
Photo Editor: Richard Fox
Design by Michele Laseau
Staff Cartographers: John Decamillis, Elizabeth Puhl, and Roberta Stockwell
Production by IDG Books Indianapolis Production Department

SPECIAL SALES

For general information on IDG Books Worldwide's books in the U.S., please call our Consumer Customer Service department at 1-800-762-2974. For reseller information, including discounts, bulk sales, customized editions, and premium sales, please call our Reseller Customer Service department at 1-800-434-3422.

Manufactured in the United States of America

5 4 3 2 1

Contents

List of Maps

AN INVITATION TO THE READER

In researching this book, we discovered many wonderful places—hotels, restaurants, shops, and more. We're sure you'll find others. Please tell us about them, so we can share the information with your fellow travelers in upcoming editions. If you were disappointed with a recommendation, we'd love to know that, too. Please write to:

Frommer's Portable Tampa & St. Petersburg, 2nd Edition
IDG Books Worldwide, Inc.
909 Third Avenue
New York, NY 10022

AN ADDITIONAL NOTE

Please be advised that travel information is subject to change at any time—and this is especially true of prices. We therefore suggest that you write or call ahead for confirmati on when making your travel plans. The authors, editors, and publisher cannot be held responsible for the experiences of readers while traveling. Your safety is important to us, however, so we encourage you to stay alert and be aware of your surroundings. Keep a close eye on cameras, purses, and wallets, all favorite targets of thieves and pickpockets.

WHAT THE SYMBOLS MEAN

✪ Frommer's Favorites

Our favorite places and experiences—outstanding for quality, value, or both.

The following abbreviations are used for credit cards:

AE	American Express	EURO	Eurocard
CB	Carte Blanche	JCB	Japan Credit Bank
DC	Diners Club	MC	MasterCard
DISC	Discover	V	Visa
ER	enRoute		

FIND FROMMER'S ONLINE

www.frommers.com offers up-to-the-minute listings on almost 200 cities around the globe—including the latest bargains and candid, personal articles updated daily by Arthur Frommer himself. No other Web site offers such comprehensive and timely coverage of the world of travel.

Planning a Trip to Tampa Bay

*M*any families visiting Orlando's theme parks eventually drive an hour west on I-4 to another major kiddie attraction, Busch Gardens Tampa Bay. But this area shouldn't be a mere side trip from Disney World, for Florida's central west coast is an exciting destination unto itself.

At the head of the bay, the city of Tampa is the commercial center of Florida's west coast—the country's 11th busiest seaport and a center of banking, high-tech manufacturing, and cigar making (half a billion drugstore stogies a year). Downtown Tampa may roll up its sidewalks after dark, but you can come here during the day to see the sea life at the Florida Aquarium and stroll through the Henry B. Plant Museum, housed in an ornate, Moorish-style hotel built a century ago to lure tourists to Tampa. A short ride will take you to Ybor City, the historic Cuban enclave that is now an exciting entertainment and dining venue. And out in the suburbs, Busch Gardens may be best known for its scintillating rides, but it's also one of the world's largest zoos.

Two bridges and a causeway will whisk you westward across the bay to the Pinellas Peninsula, one of Florida's most densely packed urban areas. Over here on the bay front, lovely downtown St. Petersburg is famous for wintering seniors, a shopping and dining complex built way out on a pier, and the world's largest collection of Salvador Dalí's surrealist paintings.

Keep driving west and you'll come to a line of barrier islands where St. Pete Beach, Treasure Island, Clearwater Beach, and other gulf-side communities boast 28 miles of sunshine, surf, and white sand. Yes, they're lined with resorts and condos of every description and price, but parks on each end preserve two of the nation's finest beaches.

Drive north up the coast, and you'll go back in time at the old Greek sponge enclave of Tarpon Springs, one of Florida's most attractive small towns, and at Weeki Wachee Springs, a tourist attraction where "mermaids" have been entertaining underwater for half a century.

Tampa & St. Petersburg

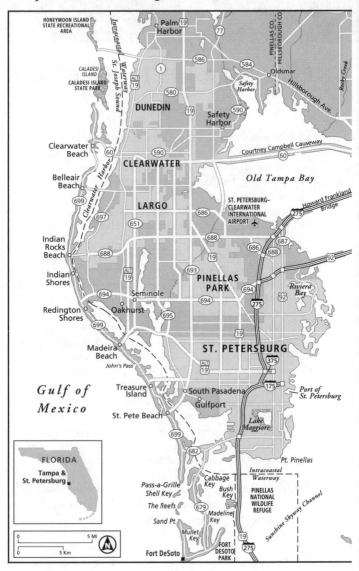

HONEYMOON ISLAND STATE RECREATIONAL AREA

CALADESI ISLAND
CALADESI ISLAND STATE PARK

Intracoastal Waterway
St. Joseph Sound

Palm Harbor

PINELLAS CO.
HILLSBOROUGH CO.

Oldsmar

Hillsborough Ave.

Rocky Creek

DUNEDIN

Safety Harbor

Safety Harbor

Clearwater Beach

Clearwater Harbor

CLEARWATER

Courtney Campbell Causeway

Belleair Beach

LARGO

ST. PETERSBURG–CLEARWATER INTERNATIONAL AIRPORT ✈

Old Tampa Bay

Howard Frankland Bridge

Indian Rocks Beach

Indian Shores

Redington Shores

Seminole

Oakhurst

PINELLAS PARK

Riviera Bay

Madeira Beach

John's Pass

St. Petersburg

Gulf of Mexico

Treasure Island

South Pasadena

Gulfport

St. Pete Beach

Lake Maggiore

Port of St. Petersburg

Pt. Pinellas

FLORIDA

Tampa & St. Petersburg

Pass-a-Grille
Shell Key

The Reefs

Sand Pt.

Cabbage Key
Bush Key

Madeline Key

Mullet Key

Fort DeSoto

FORT DESOTO PARK

Intracoastal Waterway

PINELLAS NATIONAL WILDLIFE REFUGE

Sunshine Skyway Channel

0   5 Mi
0   5 Km

N

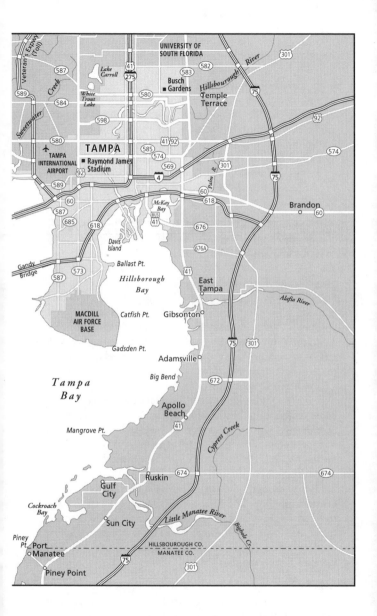

Heading south, the Sunshine Skyway will take you soaring 175 feet above the bay to Bradenton, Sarasota, and another chain of barrier islands. One of Florida's cultural centers, affluent Sarasota is the gateway to St. Armands and Longboat keys, two playgrounds of the rich and famous, and to Lido and Siesta Keys, attractive to families of more modest means. Even more reasonably priced is Anna Maria Island, off the riverfront town of Bradenton. You might say the bridge from Longboat to Anna Maria goes from one price range to another.

In this chapter you'll find the nuts and bolts to help you plan your trip to the Tampa Bay area. See the following chapters for specifics.

1 Visitor Information & Money

VISITOR INFORMATION

Your best sources for detailed information about a specific destination in Florida are the local visitor information offices. They're listed under "Orientation" or "Essentials" in the following chapters.

Contact **Visit Florida,** P.O. Box 1100, Tallahassee, FL 32302-1100 (☎ **888/7-FLA-USA;** www.flausa.com), the state's official tourism marketing agent, for a free comprehensive guide to the state. The most useful feature of this magazine-size book is a list of hotels throughout Florida.

If you're getting here by car, Visit Florida also operates **welcome centers** 16 miles west of Pensacola on I-10, 4 miles north of Jennings on I-75, 7 miles north of Yulee on I-95, and 3 miles north of Campbellton on U.S. 231. There's also a walk-in information office in the west foyer of the New Capitol Building in Tallahassee (see chapter 14).

Once you're here, you can call Visit Florida's 24-hour **tourist assistance hotline** (☎ **800/656-8777**) if you need help with lost travel documents, directions, emergencies, or references to attractions, restaurants, and shopping anywhere in the state. Hotline operators speak several languages, including Spanish, French, German, Portuguese, Japanese, and Korean.

MONEY

Traveler's checks are something of an anachronism now that you can use your credit or check cards to get cash at **automated teller machines (ATMs)** day and night. In fact, ATMs are the easiest way to get cash while you're traveling in Florida. All banks have them (with 24-hour access), and you'll find them at airports, most grocery and convenience stores, and many other locations. Most ATMs are linked to a national network that most likely includes your bank at home. **Cirrus** (☎ **800/424-7787;** www.mastercard.com/atm/) and **PLUS** (☎ **800/843-7587;** www.visa.com/atms/) are the two most popular networks; check the back of your ATM card to see which network your bank belongs to. Use the toll-free numbers to locate ATMs in your destination. Be sure to check your bank's daily withdrawal limit and your credit limits before leaving home. And don't forget: You'll need your personal identification number (PIN) to withdraw cash.

Except for the exchange desks in the major airports, including Tampa and Orlando, changing foreign currency in the United States is a hassle. Even banks here may not want to change your home currency into U.S. dollars. So leave any currency other than U.S. dollars at home, since it will prove more of a nuisance than it's worth.

2 When to Go

To a large extent, the timing of your visit will determine how much you'll spend—and how much company you'll have—once you get here. That's because room rates can more than double during the winter high season, when countless visitors migrate here.

Tampa Bay's climate is not quite sub-tropical, which means that you'll experience more extremes of temperature here than you will in places farther south, such as Miami or the Florida Keys.

Winter usually sees pleasant days and cool nights, with daytime temperatures above 70°F (21°C), with some days topping 80°F (27°C). Arctic winds can reach this far south, however, and make for brief periods of chilly days and cold nights. Bring some warm clothes just in case.

The "shoulder" seasons of **spring** and **fall**—April and May and from September to November, respectively—are great times to visit. The weather is consistently warm, and the wintertime crowds are up north enjoying their own pleasant weather.

Summer runs from June to August, when it's hot and very humid. Inland areas can be very steamy then, but the beaches

The Boys of Spring

Major-league baseball fans can watch the Tampa Bay Devil Rays in St. Petersburg throughout their season from April through September, but the entire state is a baseball hotbed from late February through March when many other teams tune up for the regular season with "Grapefruit League" exhibition games.

Most spring training stadiums are relatively small, so you can see your favorite players up close, maybe even get a handshake or an autograph. Also, tickets are priced from $5 to $12, a bargain when compared to regular season games. Many games sell out by early March, so don't wait until you get here to buy tickets.

The teams can move from year-to-year. Contact the **Florida Sports Foundation,** 2964 Wellington Circle N., Tallahassee, FL 32308 (☎ **850/488-8347;** fax 850/922-0482; www.flasports.com), or the main office of **Major League Baseball,** 350 Park Ave., New York, NY 10022 (☎ **212/339-7800;** www.majorleaguebaseball.com), to find out where your favorite teams will be playing. The schedules usually are available in January prior to the beginning of the Grapefruit League season in February.

reap the benefits of cooling breezes off the Gulf of Mexico. Severe afternoon thunderstorms are prevalent here during the summer heat, so schedule your activities for earlier in the day, and take precautions to avoid being hit by lightning during the storms.

Presidents' Day weekend in February, Easter week, Memorial Day weekend at the end of May, the Fourth of July, Labor Day weekend at the start of September, Thanksgiving, Christmas, and New Year's are busy, especially at family-oriented attractions such as Busch Gardens Tampa Bay, Walt Disney World and the other Orlando theme parks.

For up-to-the-minute climes, tune in to cable TVs **Weather Channel** (www.weather.com).

Tampa Average Temperatures in Degrees Fahrenheit

Jan	Feb	Mar	Apr	May	June	July	Aug	Sept	Oct	Nov	Dec
60	61	66	72	77	81	82	82	81	75	67	62

Here's where the teams have been playing in the Tampa Bay, Orlando, and nearby areas. See the "Outdoor Activities" sections in subsequent chapters for details.

Atlanta Braves, Lake Buena Vista, near Orlando (☎ **407/939-GAME,** 407/939-1500 or 407/939-2200; www.atlantabraves.com); **Cincinnati Reds,** Sarasota (☎ **941/954-4464** or 941/955-6501; www.cincinnatireds.com); **Cleveland Indians,** Winter Haven (☎ **863/293-3900** or 863/291-5803 www.indians.com); **Detroit Tigers,** Lakeland (☎ **941/603-6278** or 941/686-8075; www.detroittigers.com); **Houston Astros,** Kissimmee, near Orlando (☎ **407/933-2520,** 407/839-3900 or 407/933-6500; www.astros.com); **Kansas City Royals,** Davenport (☎ **863/424-2500** or 863/424-7211; www.kcroyals.com); **New York Yankees,** Tampa (☎ **813/879-2244** or 813/875-7753; www.yankees.com); **Philadelphia Phillies,** Clearwater (☎ **727/442-8496** or 215/436-1000; www.phillies.com); **Pittsburgh Pirates,** Bradenton (☎ **941/748-4610;** www.pirateball.com); **Tampa Bay Devil Rays,** St. Petersburg (☎ **727/825-3250;** www.devilrays.com); **Toronto Blue Jays,** Dunedin (☎ **800/707-8269** or 727/733-0429; www.bluejays.com).

TAMPA BAY CALENDAR OF EVENTS

January
- **Outback Bowl,** Tampa. Two top college teams kick off at Houlihan's Stadium, preceded by weeklong series events. Call ☎ **813/874-2695** for more information. Usually January 1.
- **Epiphany Celebration,** Tarpon Springs. After morning services at St. Nicholas Cathedral, young folks dive for the Epiphany cross in Spring Bayou. Call ☎ **727/937-3540** for exact dates and more information. First Saturday in January.
- **International Circus Festival and Parade,** Sarasota. Circus acts, clowns, and rides for kids honor the city's rich circus heritage. Call ☎ **941/351-8888** for more information. Day after Christmas through January.

February

- **Gasparilla Pirate Fest,** Tampa. Hundreds of boats and rowdy "pirates" invade the city, then parade along Bayshore Boulevard, showering crowds with beads and coins. Call ☎ 813/273-6495 or 813/251-4500 or visit www.gotampa.com for more information. Early February.

- **Florida State Fair,** Tampa. Despite all its development, Florida still is a major agricultural state, a status it celebrates at this huge annual exposition. There are judged competitions, botanical gardens, crafts building, carny rides, nationally known entertainers. For more information, call ☎ 800/345-FAIR or visit www.floridastatefair.com. Mid-February.

March

- **Florida Strawberry Festival,** Plant City. Country music's brightest stars entertain and overdose on strawberry shortcake in the "Winter Strawberry Capital of the World." Call ☎ 813/752-9194 for exact dates and location. First weekend in March.

April

- **Festival of States,** St. Petersburg. Since 1921 one of the South's largest civic celebrations sees national band competition, three parades, concerts, sports, and more. Call ☎ 727/898-3654 or e-mail festivalofstates@aol.com for more information and exact dates. First full week in April.

- **Highland Games and Festival,** Dunedin. Scottish band contests and Highland dancing, piping, and drumming celebrate Dunedin's Scottish heritage. Call ☎ 727/733-6240 for more information. First full week in April.

October

- **Clearwater Jazz Holiday,** Clearwater. Top jazz musicians play for 4 days and nights at bay-front Coachman Park in this free musical extravaganza. For more information and exact dates, call ☎ 727/461-0011. Mid-October.

- **Guavaween,** Tampa. Ybor City's Latin-style Halloween celebration begins with the "Mama Guava Stumble," a wacky costume parade. All-night concerts from rock to reggae. Call ☎ 813/248-3712 or visit www.gotampa.com for more information. October 31.

- ✪ **John's Pass Seafood Festival,** Madeira Beach. Tons of fish, shrimp, crab, and other seafood go down the hatch at one of

Florida's largest seafood festivals. For more information, call
☎ **727/391-7373** or visit www.gulfbeaches-tampabay.com.
Last weekend in October.

December

- **JC Penney Mixed Team Golf Classic,** Tarpon Springs. Westin Innisbrook Resort hosts mixed gender teams of top pro
golfers. Call ☎ **727/942-2000,** ext. 5393, for exact dates and
ticket prices. First week in December.

3   Health & Insurance

STAYING HEALTHY

The Tampa Bay area doesn't present any unusual health hazards
for most people. Folks with certain medical conditions such as
liver disease, diabetes, and stomach ailments, however, should
avoid eating **raw oysters,** which can carry a natural bacterium
linked to severe diarrhea, vomiting, and even fatal blood poison-
ing. If in doubt, order your oysters steamed, broiled, or fried.

The area has millions of **mosquitoes** and invisible biting **sand
flies** (known as "no-see-ums"), especially in the coastal and
marshy areas, but neither insect carries malaria or other diseases.
Keep these pests at bay with a good insect repellent.

It's especially important to protect yourself against **sunburn.**
Don't underestimate the strength of the sun's rays down here,
even in the middle of winter. And remember that children need
more protection from the sun than adults do.

If you're arriving from another country, no **inoculations** are
needed to enter the United States unless you are coming from, or
have stopped over in, areas known to be suffering from epi-
demics, particularly cholera or yellow fever.

INSURANCE

Many travelers buy insurance policies providing health and acci-
dent, trip-cancellation and -interruption, and lost-luggage protection. The coverage you should consider will depend on how
you're getting here and how much protection is already contained
in your existing credit card agreements and health insurance or
other policies. Before purchasing additional insurance, read your
agreements and policies carefully. Call your insurers or
credit/charge-card companies if you have any questions.

Among the reputable issuers of travel insurance are:

Access America (☎ 800/284-8300; www.accessamerica.com); **Travel Guard International** (☎ 800/826-1300; www.noelgroup. com); **Travel Insured International, Inc.** (☎ 800/243-3174; www.travelinsured.com); **Travelex Insurance Services** (☎ 888/ 457-4602; www.travelex-insurance.com); and **Worldwide Assistance** (☎ 800/821-2828; www.worldwideassistance.com or www. europ-assistance.com).

Scuba divers can sign up with **Divers Alert Network** (DAN) (☎ 800/446-2671 or 919/684-2948; www.diversalertnetwork.org).

4 Tips for Travelers with Special Needs

FOR TRAVELERS WITH DISABILITIES

A disability shouldn't stop anyone from traveling. There are more resources out there than ever before. For example, **Walt Disney World** in Orlando assists its guests with disabilities. Disney's many services are detailed in its *Guidebook for Guests with Disabilities*. Disney no longer mails copies prior to visits, but you can pick one up at Guest Services near the front entrance to the parks. Also, you can call ☎ **407/824-4321** for answers to any questions regarding special needs.

Nationwide resources include **Mobility International USA,** P.O. Box 10767, Eugene, OR, 97440 (☎ **541/343-1284,** voice and TDD; www.miusa.org); **Twin Peaks Press,** P.O. Box 129, Vancouver, WA 98666 (☎ **360/694-2462**), which publishes travel-related books for people with disabilities; the **Travel Information Service** (☎ 215/456-9603; www.mossresourcenet.org); and **The Society for the Advancement of Travel for the Handicapped** (SATH), 347 Fifth Ave. Suite 610, New York, NY 10016 (☎ **212/447-7284;** fax 212-725-8253; www.sath.org).

Companies offering tours for those with physical or mental disabilities include **Flying Wheels Travel,** 143 West Bridge (P.O. Box 382), Owatonna, MN 55060 (☎ **800/535-6790**); **Access Adventures** (☎ **716/889-9096**), which offers sports-related vacations; **Accessible Journeys** (☎ **800/TINGLES** or 610/ 521-0339), for slow walkers and wheelchair travelers; **The Guided Tour, Inc.** (☎ **215/782-1370**); **Wilderness Inquiry** (☎ **800/728-0719** or 612/379-3858); and **Directions Unlimited** (☎ **800/533-5343**).

FOR SENIORS

With a large population of retirees, Tampa Bay offers a wide array of activities and benefits for senior citizens. Don't be shy about asking for discounts, but always carry some kind of identification, such as a driver's license, that shows your date of birth.

Also, mention the fact that you're a senior citizen when you first make your travel reservations. For example, both **Amtrak** (☎ 800/USA-RAIL; www.amtrak.com) and **Greyhound** (☎ 800/752-4841; www.greyhound.com) offer discounts to persons over 62. And many hotels offer seniors discounts, including the **Choice Hotels** (Clarion Hotels, Quality Inns, Comfort Inns, Sleep Inns, Econo Lodges, Friendship Inns, and Rodeway Inns), which give 30% off their published rates to anyone over 50, provided you book your room through their nationwide toll-free reservations numbers (that is, not directly with the hotels or through a travel agent).

Members of the **AARP,** 601 E St. NW, Washington, DC 20049 (☎ **800/424-3410** or 202/434-2277), formerly the American Association of Retired Persons, get discounts not only on hotels but on airfares and car rentals, too.

Other helpful organizations include **National Council of Senior Citizens,** 8403 Colesville Rd., Suite 1200, Silver Spring, MD 20910 (☎ **301/578-8800**); **Mature Outlook,** P.O. Box 9390, Des Moines, IA 50306 (☎ 800/336-6330); and **Golden Companions,** P.O. Box 5249, Reno, NV 89513 (☎ **702/ 324-2227**).

Companies specializing in seniors' travel include **Grand Circle Travel,** 347 Congress St., Suite 3A, Boston, MA 02210 (☎ **800/ 221-2610** or 617/350-7500); and **SAGA International Holidays,** 222 Berkeley St., Boston, MA 02115 (☎ **800/343-0273**).

If you want something more than the average vacation or guided tour, try **Elderhostel,** 75 Federal St., Boston, MA 02110-1941 (☎ **877/426-8056;** www.elderhostel.org). On Elderhostel's escorted tours, the days are packed with seminars, lectures, and field trips, and the sightseeing is all led by academic experts. They're not luxury vacations, but they're fun and fulfilling.

FOR FAMILIES

Like the rest of Florida, the Tampa Bay Area is a great family destination, with most of its hotels and restaurants willing and eager to cater to families traveling with children. Many hotels and motels let children 17 and under stay free in their parents' room (be sure to ask when you reserve).

At the beaches, it's the exception rather than the rule for a resort not to have a children's activities program (some will even mind the youngsters while the parents enjoy a night off!). Even if they don't have a children's program of their own, most will arrange baby-sitting services.

If you call ahead before dining out, you'll see that most restaurants have some facilities for children, such as booster chairs and low-priced kids' menus.

Several books on the market offer tips to help you travel with kids. Most concentrate on the United States, but two books, *Family Travel* (Lanier Publishing International) and *How to Take Great Trips with Your Kids* (The Harvard Common Press), are full of good general advice that can apply to travel anywhere. Another reliable tome, with a worldwide focus, is *Adventuring with Children* (Foghorn Press).

Family Travel Times is published six times a year by **TWYCH** (Travel with Your Children) (☎ **888-822-4388** or 212/477-5524), and includes a weekly call-in service for subscribers. Subscriptions are $40 a year for quarterly editions. A free publication list and a sample issue are available by calling or sending a request to the above address.

Families Welcome!, 92 N. Main, Ashland, OR 97520 (☎ **800/326-0724** or 541/482-6121), is a travel company specializing in worry-free vacations for families.

FOR STUDENTS

It's worthwhile to bring along your valid high school or college identification. Presenting it can mean discounted admission to museums and other attractions. And remember, alcoholic beverages cannot be sold in Florida to anyone who is under 21, so if you're eligible and intend to imbibe, bring your driver's license or another valid photo identification showing your date of birth.

FOR GAY & LESBIAN TRAVELERS

Tampa Bay is not as widely known as a gay-friendly destination as are others in Florida, such as Orlando, Key West, and Miami's South Beach. The popularity of Orlando with gay and lesbian travelers is highlighted with Gay Weekend in early June, which draws as many as 40,000 participants and includes events at

Disney World, Universal Studios, and Sea World. You can get information on the event at *www.gayday.com* or *www.gaydays.com*. **Universal City Travel** (☎ 800/224-3838), offers a "Gay Weekend" tour package including tickets to Universal Studios, Sea World, and Church Street Station. For information about events for that weekend, or throughout the year, contact the **Gay, Lesbian & Bisexual Community Services of Central Florida,** 934 N. Mills Ave., Orlando, FL 32803 (☎ 407/425-4527 or 407/843-4297; www.glbcc.org). *Watermark,* P.O. Box 533655, Orlando, FL 32853 (☎ 407/481-2243; fax 407/481-2246; www.watermarkonline.com), is a biweekly tabloid newspaper covering the gay and lesbian scene, including dining and entertainment options, in Orlando and the Tampa Bay Area.

National resources include *Out and About,* 8 W. 19th St. #401, New York, NY 10011 (☎ 800/929-2268 or 212/645-6922), which offers guidebooks and a monthly newsletter packed with good information on the global gay and lesbian scene; and *Our World,* 1104 North Nova Rd., Suite 251, Daytona Beach, FL 32117 (☎ 904/441-5367), a monthly magazine promoting and highlighting travel bargains and opportunities.

The International Gay & Lesbian Travel Association (IGLTA), (☎ 800/448-8550 or 954/776-2626; fax 954/776-3303; www.iglta.org), links travelers up with the appropriate gay-friendly service organization or tour specialist. General gay and lesbian travel agencies include **Family Abroad** (☎ 800/999-5500 or 212/459-1800; gay and lesbian); **Above and Beyond Tours** (☎ 800/397-2681; mainly gay men); and **Yellowbrick Road** (☎ 800/642-2488; gay and lesbian).

5 Getting There & Getting Around

BY PLANE

The area's major air gateway is **Tampa International Airport,** 5 miles northwest of downtown Tampa (see chapter 2). Most major and many no-frills airlines fly here, including **Air Canada** (☎ 800/268-7240 in Canada, 800/776-3000 in the United States), **AirTran** (☎ 800/AIR-TRAN); **American** (☎ 800/433-7300), **America West** (☎ 800/235-9292), **British Airways** (☎ 800/247-9297), **Cayman Airways** (☎ 800/422-9626), **Canadian Airlines International** (☎ 800/426-7000),

Continental (☎ 800/525-0280), **Delta** (☎ 800/221-1212), **MetroJet,** (☎ 800/428-4322); **Midway** (☎ 800/446-4392), **Midwest Express** (☎ 800/452-2022); **Northwest/KLM** (☎ 800/225-2525), **Spirit** (☎ 800/ 722-7117); **Southwest** (☎ 800/435-9792), **TWA** (☎ 800/221-2000), **United** (☎ 800/ 241-6522), and **US Airways** (☎ 800/428-4322).

Alamo (☎ 800/327-9633), **Avis** (☎ 800/331-1212), **Budget** (☎ 800/527-0700), **Dollar** (☎ 800/800-4000), **Enterprise** (☎ 800/325-8007), **Hertz** (☎ 800/654-3131), **National** (☎ 800/CAR-RENT), and **Thrifty** (☎ 800/367-2277) all have rental-car operations here.

SuperShuttle (☎ **800/BLUE-VAN**) operates van services between the airport and hotels throughout the Tampa Bay area. Fares for one person vary considerably depending on where you're going. One passenger will pay at least $6 to Tampa's downtown or West Shore area, $13 to Busch Gardens, downtown St. Petersburg, the beaches, or Tarpon Springs. **Taxis** are plentiful at the airport; the ride to downtown Tampa takes about 15 minutes and costs $11 to $14.

There is limited service to **St. Petersburg–Clearwater International Airport** (see "Orientation" in chapter 3).

Sarasota–Bradenton International Airport, off U.S. 41 and U.S. 301 between the two cities (see "Orientation" in chapter 7), is served by **American** (☎ 800/433-7300), **America Trans Air** (☎ 800/225-2995), **Canada 3000** (☎ 800/993-4378), **Continental** (☎ 800/525-0280), **Delta** (☎ 800/221-1212), **Northwest/KLM** (☎ 800/225-2525), **TWA** (☎ 800/ 221-2000), and **US Airways** (☎ 800/428-4322).

There's no shortage of **discounted and promotional fares** to Tampa Bay. November, December, and January often see fare wars that can result in savings of 50% or more. Watch for advertisements in your local newspaper and on TV, or call the airlines.

Ask the airlines for their lowest fares, and ask if it's cheaper to book in advance, fly in midweek, or stay over a Saturday night. Decide when you want to go before you call, since many of the best deals are nonrefundable.

Many **charter flights** fly here, especially during the winter season. They cost less than regularly scheduled flights, but they are very complicated. Go to a good travel agent and ask him or her to find one for you and to explain the problems as well as the advantages.

BY CAR

If you're driving from Orlando and other points east, take I-4, which dead-ends in downtown Tampa. I-75 is this area's major north-south route, with I-275 running more or less parallel to it from northern Tampa through St. Petersburg and across the bay to Bradenton and Sarasota. U.S. 19, U.S. 41, and U.S. 301 also are other major north-south arteries here, but they are infested with stoplights and are usually clogged at rush-hour, as is U.S. 90 and Fla. 60, which run east-west through Tampa and St. Petersburg.

If you're a member, your local branch of the **American Automobile Association (AAA)** will provide a free trip-routing plan. AAA also has nationwide emergency road service (☎ **800/ AAA-HELP**).

If you decide to rent a car (see "By Plane," above), shop around and ask a lot of questions, since rates and special deals change constantly, and the rental firms certainly aren't going to volunteer to save you money. If you belong to an organization such as AARP or AAA, check to see if you get a discount.

BY TRAIN

Amtrak (☎ **800/USA-RAIL;** www.amtrak.com) runs its *Silver Palm* daily between New York and Tampa. From there you can take a Thruway Bus Connection to St. Petersburg, Treasure Island, Clearwater, Tarpon Springs, Bradenton, and Sarasota. The *Sunset Limited* runs three times weekly between Los Angeles and Orlando, with bus connections on to Tampa. Sleeping accommodations are available on both trains for an extra charge.

Frankly, Amtrak's fares aren't much less than many deals offered by the airlines. If you intend to stop off along the way, you can save money with its **Explore America** (or All Aboard America) fares, which are based on three regions of the country.

Amtrak's **Auto Train** runs daily from Lorton, Virginia (12 miles south of Washington, D.C.), to Sanford, Florida (just northeast of Orlando, about an hour's drive from Tampa). You ride in a coach while your car is secured in an enclosed vehicle carrier. Make your Auto Train reservations as far in advance as possible.

6 Package Tours

Travel agents offer hundreds of package tour options to Florida. Quite often a package tour will result in savings not just on airfares but on hotels and other activities as well. Airfare, transfers, and accommodations are always covered, and sometimes meals and specific activities are thrown in. Ask your travel agent to find the best package tours to Tampa Bay.

The major airlines package their flights to Florida together with accommodations. These include **America West Vacations** (☎ 800/356-6611; fax 602/3505), **American Airlines Vacations** (☎ 800/321-2121 fax 800/472-2987; www.americanair.com), **Continental Airlines Vacations** (☎ 800/634-5555; fax 954/357-4661; www.flycontinental.com), **Delta Vacations** (☎ 800/367-9112; fax 954/468-4765; www.deltavacations.com), **Midwest Express Vacations** (☎ 800/444-4479; fax 414/351-5256), **Northwest WorldVacations** (☎ 800/727-1111; fax 800/655-7890; www.deltavacations.com), **Southwest Airlines Vacations** (☎ 800/524-6442; fax 407/857-0232; www.iflyswa.com), and **US Airways Vacations** (☎ 800/455-0123).

Another option is the old, reliable **American Express Vacations** (☎ **800/241-1700;** fax 954/357-4682). Check out the on AmEx's Web site (http://travel.americanexpress.com) for last-minute travel bargains, deeply discounted vacations packages and reduced airline fares. **Northwest Airlines** (www.nwa.com) posts "Cyber Saver Bargain Alerts" on its Web site weekly, offering special hotel rates, package deals, and discounted airline fares.

There are some drawbacks: The least expensive tours may put you up at a bottom-end hotel. And since the lower costs depend on volume, some more expensive tours could send you to a large, impersonal property. And since the tour prices are based on double occupancy, the single traveler is almost invariably penalized.

In Orlando, the **Walt Disney World Central Reservations Office** (☎ **407/W-DISNEY**) and **Universal City Travel Co.** (☎ **800/224-3838**) both have numerous packages including air, hotel, and discounted admissions.

In addition to these all-inclusive tours, many hotels and resorts and even some motels here offer **golf and tennis packages,** which bundle the cost of room, greens and court fees, and sometimes equipment into one price. These deals usually don't include airfare, but they do represent savings over paying for the room and golf or tennis separately. See the accommodations sections in the following chapters for hostelries offering special packages to their guests.

7 Tips on Accommodations

The Tampa Bay area has a vast array of accommodations, from rock-bottom roadside motels to one of the nation's finest resorts. Whether you spend a pittance or a bundle depends on your budget and your tastes. In the words of that well-worn phrase, you can enjoy "champagne on a beer budget"—if you plan carefully.

The annual trip-planning guide published by the state's tourism promotion agency, **Visit Florida** (see "Visitor Information," above), lists most hotels and motels in the state. It's particularly handy if you're taking your animal along, since it tells whether they accept pets.

Another excellent source is ○ **Superior Small Lodgings**, a national organization of quality hotels, motels, and inns. None of these properties has more than 75 rooms, and all have been inspected for cleanliness, quality, comfort, privacy, and safety. Contact the local tourist information offices for lists of members in their areas, or the **Florida Superior Small Lodging Association,** 926 Elysium Blvd., Mount Dora, FL 32757 (☎ **352/735-4635;** fax 352/735-3944; www.SuperiorSmallLodging.com). Many hotels and motels recommended in this book are members.

Inn Route, P.O. Box 6187, Palm Harbor, FL 34684 (☎ **800/524-1880;** fax 281/403-9335; www.florida-inns.com; e-mail: innroute@worldnet.att.net), publishes the *Inns of Florida,* which lists inns and bed-and-breakfasts throughout the state. Inn Route also inspects each property, thus ensuring quality and cleanliness of its members.

MONEY-SAVING TIPS

The rates quoted in this book are "rack" or "published" rates; that is, the highest regular rates charged by a hotel or motel. That used to be what you paid unless you were part of a tour group or had purchased a vacation package, but today most hotels give discounts to corporate travelers, government employees, senior citizens, automobile club members, active duty military personnel, and others. Most usually don't advertise these discounted rates or even volunteer them at the front desk, but you can take advantage of them by asking politely if there's a special rate that applies to you.

Computerized reservations systems also have permitted many larger properties to adjust their rates almost daily, depending on how much business they anticipate having. Even if they don't officially reduce their rates, they may drop them rather than having beds go empty. Don't hesitate to ask if a less expensive rate is available on the days you plan on being there.

Most rack rates include commissions of 10% to 25% or more for travel agents, which many hotels will knock off if you make your own reservations and bargain a little.

You're probably better off dealing directly with a hotel, but, if you don't like bargaining, check out one of the national **reservation services.** They usually work as consolidators, buying up or reserving rooms in bulk, and then dealing them out to customers at a profit. Most of them offer online reservation services as well. The more reputable providers include **Accommodations Express** (☎ **800/950-4685;** www. accommodationsxpress.com); **Hotel Reservations Network** (☎ **800/96HOTEL;** www.180096HOTEL.com); **Quikbook** (☎ **800/789-9887,** includes fax on demand service; www. quikbook.com); and **Room Exchange** (☎ **800/846-7000** in the United States, 800/486-7000 in Canada; www. hotelrooms.com).

Online, try booking your hotel through **Arthur Frommer's Budget Travel** (www.frommers.com), and save up to 50% off the rack rate. **Microsoft Expedia** (www.expedia.com) features a "Travel Agent" that will also direct you to affordable lodgings.

Hotels in downtown Tampa, which cater primarily to business travelers during the week, often have big discounts on Friday and Saturday nights. Weekend rates don't apply at the beaches, but you should ask there about weekday or week-long vacation packages.

Most hotels also have free self-parking, but fees can run up the cost at some downtown and beachfront hotels. I've indicated in the listings if a hotel or resort charges for parking; if no charge is given, parking is free. And many hotels jack up the price of long-distance phone calls made from your room. Accordingly, always inquire about the costs of parking, and use a pay phone if the hotel tacks a hefty surcharge on calls.

CONDOS, HOMES & COTTAGES

It may seem at first impression that many Tampa Bay beaches are lined with great walls of high-rise condominium buildings. That's not much of an overstatement, for the area literally has thousands of condo units. People actually live in many of them year-round, but others are for rent on a daily, weekly, or monthly basis. In addition, there are many private homes and cottages for rent.

Be aware, however, that in Florida real estate and resort parlance, the word *villa* does not mean a luxurious house standing all by itself. Down here, "villa" means an apartment.

Some of the resorts listed in this book actually are condo complexes operated as full-service hotels, but usually you'll have to without such hotel amenities as on-site restaurants, room service, and even daily maid service. On the other hand, almost every condo, home, and cottage has a fully equipped kitchen, and many have washers, dryers, and other such niceties of home, which means they can represent significant savings, especially if you're traveling with children or are sharing with another couple or family.

I have pointed out some of the best condo complexes in the "Where to Stay" sections of the following chapters, and I have named some of the reputable **real estate agencies** that have inventories of condos, private homes, and cottages to rent.

If you think a condo will meet your needs, your best bet is to contact the rental agencies well in advance and request a brochure describing all the properties they represent, and their rates.

FAST FACTS: TAMPA BAY

American Express   There are American Express offices in Tampa (☎ 813/273-0310), St. Petersburg (☎ 813/577-5282), and Sarasota (☎ 941/923-7579). Call Cardmember Services (☎ 800/528-4800) for other locations.

Banks   Banks are usually open Monday to Friday from 9am to 3 or 4pm, and most have automated teller machines (ATMs) for 24-hour banking. You won't have a problem finding a Cirrus or PLUS machine (see "Visitor Information & Money," above). Of the national banks, **First Union Bank** and **NationsBank** have offices throughout Florida. **Barnett** and **Sun** are the largest in-state banks.

Car Rentals   See "Getting There & Getting Around," earlier in this chapter.

Climate   See "When to Go," earlier in this chapter.

Currency Exchange   See "Visitor Information & Money," above.

Emergencies   Call **911** anywhere in Florida to summon the police, the fire department, or an ambulance.

Liquor Laws   You must be 21 to purchase or consume alcohol anywhere in Florida. This law is strictly enforced, so if you look young, carry some photo identification that gives your date of birth. Minors can usually enter bars where food is served.

Newspapers/Magazines   The top local newspapers here are the *Tampa Tribune* and the *St. Petersburg Times*. The well-respected *Miami Herald* is generally available all over the state.

Safety   Whenever you're traveling in an unfamiliar city, stay alert. Be aware of your immediate surroundings. Always lock your car doors and the trunk when your vehicle is unattended, and don't leave any valuables in sight.

Taxes   The Florida state sales tax is 6%. Many municipalities add 1% or more to that, and most levy a special tax on hotel and restaurant bills. See "Where to Stay" in the following chapters for details.

Time   Tampa Bay observes eastern standard time.

Tourist Information   See "Visitor Information & Money," earlier in this chapter, for the tourist office serving the entire state. For local offices, which will have more detailed information on your particular destination, see "Orientation" in the following chapters.

Tampa

*E*ven if you stay at the beaches 20 miles to the west, you should consider driving into Tampa to see its sights. If you have children in tow, they will *demand* that you go into the city so they can ride the rides and see the animals at Busch Gardens. While here, you can educate them at the Florida Aquarium and the city's fine museums. And if you don't have kids, historic Ybor City has the bay area's liveliest nightlife.

Tampa was a sleepy little port when Cuban immigrants founded Ybor City's cigar industry in the 1880s. A few years later Henry B. Plant put Tampa on the tourist map by building a railroad to town and the bulbous minarets over his garish Tampa Bay Hotel, now a museum named in his honor. During the Spanish American War, Teddy Roosevelt trained his Rough Riders here and walked the Ybor City streets with Cuban revolutionary José Marti. A land boom in the 1920s gave the city its charming, Victorian-style Hyde Park suburb, now a gentrified redoubt of the baby boomers just across the Hillsborough River from downtown.

Today's downtown skyline is the product of the 1980s and early 1990s boom, when banks built skyscrapers and the city put up an expansive convention center, a performing arts center, and the Ice Palace, a 20,000-seat bay-front arena that is home to professional hockey's Tampa Bay Lightning. Alongside the new Florida Aquarium, the Garrison Seaport Center is a major home port for cruise ships bound for Mexico and the Caribbean. Baseball's New York Yankees helped things along by building their spring training complex here, including a scaled-down replica of Yankee Stadium. And the sparkling Raymond James Stadium became the home to pro football's Tampa Bay Buccaneers in 1998.

You won't want to spend your entire vacation here, but all this adds up to a fast-paced, modern city on the go.

1 Orientation

ARRIVING

Tampa is accessible via I-275, I-75, I-4, U.S. 19, U.S. 41, U.S. 92, and U.S. 301. The Busch Gardens area lies between I-75 and I-275 north of downtown; exit at Busch Boulevard and follow the signs. Downtown is south of I-275; take Exit 26 and go south on Ashley Street.

Tampa International Airport, off Memorial Highway and Fla. 60, 5 miles northwest of downtown Tampa, is the major air gateway to this area. All of the major car rental firms have booths at or near the airport, and **SuperShuttle** (☎ 800/BLUE-VAN) operates van services between the airport and hotels throughout the Tampa Bay area. See "Getting There & Getting Around" in chapter 1 for details.

Local **HARTline buses** stop in front of the red baggage claim area (see "Getting Around," below). There's a sign posted there with a route map. Rides cost $1.15 for local buses, $1.50 for express service. Exact is change required.

Amtrak trains arrive downtown at the **Tampa Amtrak Station,** 601 Nebraska Ave. N. (☎ 800/USA-RAIL).

VISITOR INFORMATION

Contact the **Tampa/Hillsborough Convention and Visitors Association (THCVA),** 400 N. Tampa St., Tampa, FL 33602-4706 (☎ 800/44-TAMPA or 813/223-2752; fax 813/229-6616; www.gotampa.com) for advance information. Once you're downtown, head to the THCVA's visitors information center at the corner of Ashley and Madison streets. It's open Monday to Saturday from 9am to 5pm.

The **Ybor City Chamber of Commerce** has a visitors center in an old cigar-roller's cottage at 1800 E. 9th Ave. (at 18th St.), Tampa, FL 33605 (☎ 877/934-3782 or 813/248-3712; fax 813/247-1764; www.ybor.org). Open Monday to Friday from 9am to 5pm.

Near Busch Gardens, the privately owned **Tampa Bay Visitor Information Center,** 3601 E. Busch Blvd., at N. Ednam Place (☎ 813/985-3601; fax 813/985-7642), offers free brochures about attractions in Tampa and sells discounted tickets to many attractions. You may be able to both save $2 a head and avoid waiting in long ticket lines at Busch Gardens by buying here. Owner Jim

Boggs worked for the park for many years and gives expert advice about how to get the most out of your visit, and he will book hotel rooms and car rentals for you, often at a discount. Open Monday to Saturday from 9am to 5:30pm, Sunday from 9am to 2pm. Operating as Swiss Chalet Tours, this same company also has organized excursions of the area (see "Organized Tours," below).

2 Getting Around

Like most other Florida destinations, it's virtually impossible to see Tampa's major sights and enjoy the best restaurants without a car.

In the works at press time, a street car-on-rails is planned to haul passengers between downtown and Ybor City, perhaps in 2001. It is expected to travel by the Florida Aquarium. Check with the visitors center (see above), or call the **Hillsborough Area Regional Transit/HARTline** (☎ 813/254-HART; www. hartline.org).

If you're on a budget, HARTline also provides regularly scheduled **bus service** between downtown Tampa and the suburbs. Pick up a route map at the visitors information center (see above).

Taxis in Tampa don't normally cruise the streets for fares, but they do line up at public loading places, such as hotels, the performing arts center, and bus and train depots. If you need a taxi, call **Tampa Bay Cab** (☎ 813/251-5555), **Yellow Cab** (☎ 813/253-0121), or **United Cab** (☎ 813/253-2424). Fares are 95¢ at flag fall plus $1.50 for each mile.

3 Exploring Tampa

THEME & ANIMAL PARKS

Adventure Island. 10001 McKinley Dr. (between Busch Blvd. and Bougainvillea Ave.). ☎ 813/987-5600. www.adventureisland.com. Admission and hours vary from year to year so call ahead, check Web site, or get brochure at visitors centers. Admission at least $23.95 adults, $21.95 children 3–9, plus tax. Free for children 2 and under. Seasonal passes and combination tickets with Busch Gardens Tampa Bay and SeaWorld Florida in Orlando available. Late Feb to Labor Day daily 10am–5pm; Sept–Oct Fri–Sun 10am–5pm (extended hours in summer and on holidays). Closed Nov to late Feb. Take Exit 33 off I-275, go east on Busch Blvd. for 2 miles, turn left onto McKinley Dr. (N. 40th St.), and entry is on right.

If the summer heat gets to you before one of Tampa's famous thunderstorms brings late-afternoon relief, you can take a waterlogged

Tampa Attractions

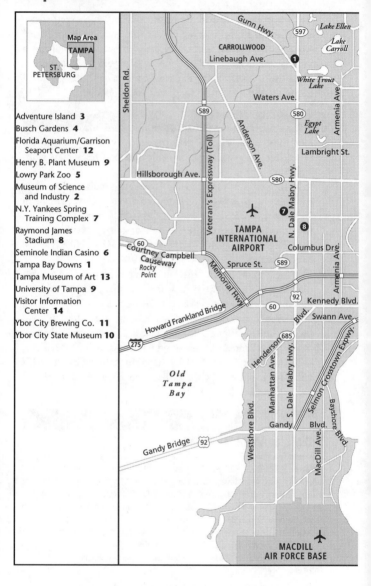

Map Area
TAMPA

ST. PETERSBURG

Adventure Island **3**

Busch Gardens **4**

Florida Aquarium/Garrison Seaport Center **12**

Henry B. Plant Museum **9**

Lowry Park Zoo **5**

Museum of Science and Industry **2**

N.Y. Yankees Spring Training Complex **7**

Raymond James Stadium **8**

Seminole Indian Casino **6**

Tampa Bay Downs **1**

Tampa Museum of Art **13**

University of Tampa **9**

Visitor Information Center **14**

Ybor City Brewing Co. **11**

Ybor City State Museum **10**

Gunn Hwy.

597

Lake Ellen

Lake Carroll

CARROLLWOOD

Linebaugh Ave.

White Trout Lake

Waters Ave.

Armenia Ave.

Sheldon Rd.

589

580

Egypt Lake

Anderson Ave.

Lambright St.

Hillsborough Ave.

580

N. Dale Mabry Hwy.

Veteran's Expressway (Toll)

TAMPA INTERNATIONAL AIRPORT

Columbus Dr.

60

Courtney Campbell Causeway

Rocky Point

Spruce St.

589

Memorial Hwy.

Armenia Ave.

92

Kennedy Blvd.

60

Swann Ave.

Howard Frankland Bridge

275

Old Tampa Bay

Westshore Blvd.

Henderson Blvd.

Manhattan Ave.

S. Dale Mabry Hwy.

685

Selmon Crosstown Expwy.

Bayshore Blvd.

Gandy

Blvd.

MacDill Ave.

Gandy Bridge

92

MACDILL AIR FORCE BASE

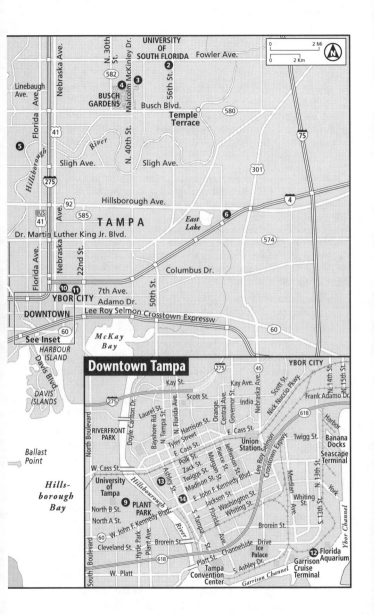

Map labels (main map, top to bottom, left to right):

Linebaugh Ave.
Nebraska Ave.
N. 30th St.
Malcolm McKinley Dr.
UNIVERSITY OF SOUTH FLORIDA
Fowler Ave.
2
56th St.
582
4
3
BUSCH GARDENS
Busch Blvd.
580
Temple Terrace
Florida Ave.
41
75
5
Hillsborough River
N. 40th St.
Sligh Ave.
Sligh Ave.
275
92
Hillsborough Ave.
301
BUS 41
585
T A M P A
East Lake
6
574
Nebraska Ave.
Dr. Martin Luther King Jr. Blvd.
4
22nd St.
Columbus Dr.
50th St.
Florida Ave.
10 **11**
7th Ave.
YBOR CITY
Adamo Dr.
Lee Roy Selmon Crosstown Expressw.
DOWNTOWN
60
60
See Inset
HARBOUR ISLAND
McKay Bay
Davis Blvd
DAVIS ISLANDS
Ballast Point
Hills-borough Bay

Scale bar: 0 — 2 Mi / 0 — 2 Km

Downtown Tampa inset labels:

YBOR CITY
275
45
Kay St.
Kay Ave.
India
Scott St.
Scott St.
Nick Nuccio Pkwy.
N. 14th St.
N. 15th St.
Frank Adamo Dr.
618
275
Doyle Carlton Dr.
Laurel St.
Bayshore Rd.
N. Tampa Ave.
N. Florida Ave.
N. Harrison St.
Orange
Central Ave.
Governor St.
Nebraska Ave.
E. Cass St.
Scott St.
Harbor
RIVERFRONT PARK
Tyler Street
E. Cass St.
Polk St.
Zack St.
Union Station
Twigg St.
Banana Docks
Seascape Terminal
W. Cass St.
Ashley St.
Twiggs St.
Morgan St.
Pierce St.
Jefferson St.
Lee Roy Selmon Crosstown Expwy.
N. 13th St.
S. 13th St.
York
Hillsborough
Madison St.
13
E. John F. Kennedy Blvd.
Jackson St.
Whiting St.
Meridian Ave.
Whiting St.
University of Tampa
9
PLANT PARK
North B St.
North A St.
W. John F. Kennedy Blvd.
14
Washington St.
Brorein St.
Ybor Channel
Hillsborough Bay
60
Hyde Park Ave.
Plant Ave.
River
S. Tampa Ave.
Florida Ave.
South Boulevard
Cleveland St.
Brorein St.
Channelside Dr.
Drive Ice Palace
618
W. Platt
Platt St.
S. Ashley Dr.
Tampa Convention Center
Garrison Cruise Terminal
12
Florida Aquarium
Garrison Channel

break at this 25-acre outdoor water theme park near Busch
Gardens Tampa Bay (see below). In fact, you can frolic here even
during the cooler days of spring and fall, when the water is heated.
The Key West Rapids, Tampa Typhoon, Gulf Scream, and other
exciting water rides will drench the teens, while other calmer rides
are geared for kids. There are places to picnic and sunbathe, a
games arcade, a volleyball complex, and an outdoor cafe. If you
forget to bring your own, a surf shop sells bathing suits, towels, and
suntan lotion.

✪ Busch Gardens Tampa Bay. 3000 E. Busch Blvd. (at McKinley Dr./
N. 40th St.). ☎ **813/987-5283.** www.buschgardens.com. Admission and
hours vary so call ahead, check Web site, or get brochure at visitors centers.
Admission $43.70 adults, $37.70 children 3–9, plus tax. Free for children 2 and
under. Seasonal passes and combination tickets with Adventure Island and Sea-
World Florida in Orlando available. Daily 10am–6pm (extended hours to 7 and
8pm in the summer and holidays). Parking $6. Take I-275 north of downtown
to Busch Blvd. (Exit 33), and go east 2 miles. From I-75, take Fowler Ave. (Exit
54) and follow the signs west.

Although its thrill rides, live entertainment, shops, restaurants,
and games get most of the ink, this venerable theme park (it pre-
dates Disney World) ranks among the top zoos in the country.
This is a great place for the kids to see in person all those wild
beasts they've watched on the Discovery Channel—and you'll be
closer to them here than at Disney's Animal Kingdom in Orlando
(see chapter 12). The animals—several thousand of them—live in
naturalistic environments and help carry out an overall African
and Egyptian theme.

The park is divided into eight areas, each with its own theme,
animals, live entertainment, thrill rides, kiddie attractions,
dining, and shopping. A Skyride cable car soars over the park,
offering a bird's-eye view of the park.

Allow at least a day here, and arrive early—but try not to come
when it's raining, since some rides may not operate and you won't
get a rain check for free admission on another day (but you can
buy a ticket inside the park for a second day's admission for $12
per person). Bring comfortable shoes, and remember, you can get
wet on some of the rides, so wear appropriate clothing.

You can avoid waiting in long lines, and save a few dollars, by
buying your tickets in advance at the **Tampa Bay Visitor Information Center** near the main entrance (see "Essentials," above).
You can exchange foreign currency in the park, and interpreters
are available.

As soon as you're through the turnstiles, pick up a copy of a park map and the day's activity schedule, which tells what's showing and when at the park's 14 entertainment venues. Then take a few minutes to carefully plan your time—it's a big park with lots to see and do. Busch Gardens continues to grow, so be on the lookout for new attractions.

Just past the main gate you'll come to **Morocco,** a walled city with exotic architecture, craft demonstrations, a sultan's tent with snake charmers, and an exhibit featuring alligators and turtles. The Moroccan Palace Theater features an ice show, which many families consider to be the park's best entertainment for both adults and children. Here you can also attend a song and dance show in the Marrakech Theater.

After watching the snake charmers in Morocco, walk eastward to **Egypt,** where you can see Anheuser-Busch's fabled Clydesdale horses, visit King Tut's tomb, and listen to comedian Martin Short narrate "Akbar's Adventure Tours," a wacky simulator that "transports" one and all across Egypt via camel, biplane, and mine car. Adults and older kids can ride Montu, the tallest and longest inverted roller coaster in the world with seven upside-down loops, one of them barely missing a crocodile pit. Youngsters can dig for their own ancient treasures in a sand area.

From Egypt, walk onto the **Edge of Africa,** the most unique part of the park. Here glass walls separate you from lions, hippos, crocodiles, hyenas, meerkats, and vultures among more than 500 African animals roaming freely on an 80-acre natural grassy veldt known here as the Serengeti Plain.

Next stop is **Nairobi,** where you can see gorillas and chimpanzees in the Myombe Reserve, replicating their natural tropical habitat. Nairobi also has a baby animal nursery, a petting zoo, turtle and reptile displays, an elephant exhibit, and Curiosity Caverns, a simulated environment that allows you to observe animals that are active in the dark.

From Nairobi, walk into **Timbuktu,** evoking an ancient desert trading center with African craftspeople at work. Here you'll find several rides, including The Sandstorm, the Phoenix, and the Scorpion, a 360° roller coaster. Plan to have lunch here at Das Festhaus, a 1,200-seat, air-conditioned German festival hall featuring a lively musical show "The International Celebration" (be sure to arrive at least 15 minutes before show time to get a seat). The kids will enjoy the Dolphin Theater, with performing porpoises, otters, and sea lions.

After lunch, head to **The Congo,** highlighted by rare white Bengal tigers living on Claw Island. The Congo also is home to two roller coasters: the Kumba, the largest and fastest roller coaster in the southeastern United States; and the Python, which twists and turns for 1,200 feet. You will get drenched (and refreshed on a hot day) by riding the Congo River Rapids. There are bumper cars and kiddie rides here, too.

From The Congo, walk south into **Stanleyville,** a prototype African village, with a shopping bazaar, orangutans living on an island, and the Stanleyville Theater, usually featuring shows for children. Two more water rides are here: the Tanganyika Tidal Wave and Stanley Falls. Serving ribs and chicken, the Stanleyville Smokehouse has some of the best chow here. This also is a good place to board the Trans-veldt Railway for a sightseeing ride all the way around the park and back, since you'll avoid the crowds waiting to board elsewhere.

From Stanleyville, the next stop is **Land of the Dragons,** where the younger set can easily spend an entire day enjoying a variety of play elements in a fairy-tale setting, plus just-for-kids rides. The area is dominated by Dumphrey, a whimsical dragon who interacts with visitors and guides children around a three-story tree house with winding stairways, tall towers, stepping stones, illuminated water geysers, and an echo chamber.

The next stop is **Bird Gardens,** the park's original core, offering rich foliage, lagoons, and a free-flight aviary for hundreds of exotic birds, including golden and American bald eagles. Catch the Bird Show here, and be sure to see the Florida flamingos and Australian koalas.

Next take a break at the **Hospitality House,** which offers piano entertainment and free samples of Anheuser-Busch's famous beers. You must be 21 to imbibe (there's a limit of two free mugs per seating), but soft drinks also are available.

If your stomach can take another hair-raising ride, the last stop is at **Gwazi,** the park's newest village. The highlight here is a pair of old-fashion wooden roller coasters named the Lion and the Tiger, which start simultaneously and whiz within a few feet of each other six times as they roar along at 50 m.p.h. Since the coasters rise to "only" 90 feet (that's low compared to the park's other thrillers), most family members can give them a go. In Gwazi's "Water Wars," participants shoot water-filled balloons at each other with big slingshots. It's a soaking way to end your visit.

✪ **The Florida Aquarium.** 701 Channelside Dr. ☎ **813/273-4000.** www.flaquarium.net. Admission $11.95 adults, $10.95 seniors, $6.95 children 3–12, free for children under 3. Parking $3. Daily 9:30am–5pm. Closed Thanksgiving and Christmas.

You'll be introduced to more than 5,000 aquatic animals and plants that call Florida home at this entertaining and informative aquarium. The exhibits follow a drop of water from the pristine springs of the Florida Wetlands Gallery, through a mangrove forest in the Bays and Beaches Gallery, and out onto the Coral Reefs, where an impressive 43-foot-wide, 14-foot-tall panoramic window lets you look out to schools of fish and lots of sharks and stingrays. There's a half-million-dollar "Explore a Shore" playground to educate the kids, a deep-water exhibit, and a tank housing moray eels. Florida sea life is not all you'll see here, for a special Dragons Down Under exhibit features rare sea dragons (it's difficult to tell if they're seahorses or seaweed) and other creatures from Australia. The Cafe Ray serves snacks and light meals.

Lowry Park Zoo. 7530 North Blvd. ☎ **813/935-8552** or 813/932-0245 for recorded information. Admission $8.50 adults, $7.50 seniors, $4.95 children 3–11, free for children 2 and under. Daily 9:30am–4:45pm. Closed Thanksgiving and Christmas. Take I-275 to Sligh Ave. (Exit 31) and follow the signs.

Watching 2,000-pound manatees, komodo dragons, and rare red pandas makes this a worthwhile excursion after the kids have seen the plains of Africa at Busch Gardens. With lots of greenery, bubbling brooks, and cascading waterfalls, this 24-acre zoo displays animals in settings similar to their natural habitats. Other major exhibits include a Florida wildlife display, an Asian Domain, a Primate World, an Aquatic Center, a free-flight aviary with a birds of prey show, a children's petting zoo and hands-on Discovery Center, and an endangered species carrousel ride. There are plenty of food outlets here, including an on-site McDonald's.

VISITING THE MUSEUMS

Henry B. Plant Museum. 401 W. Kennedy Blvd. (between Hyde Park and Magnolia aves.). ☎ **813/254-1891.** www.plantmuseum.com. Free admission; suggested donation $5 adults, $1 children 12 and under. Tues–Sat 10am–4pm, Sun noon–4pm. Take Kennedy Blvd. (Fla. 60) across Hillsborough River.

Originally built in 1891 by railroad tycoon Henry B. Plant as the 511-room Tampa Bay Hotel, this ornate building alone is worth a short trip across the river from downtown. Its 13 silver minarets and distinctive Moorish architecture, modeled after the Alhambra in Spain, make this National Historic Landmark a focal point of the Tampa skyline. It's filled with art and furnishings from Europe and the Orient, and exhibits explain the history of the original railroad resort, Florida's early tourist industry, and the hotel's role as a staging point for Teddy Roosevelt's Rough Riders during the Spanish American War. Call for a schedule of special exhibits.

✪ **Museum of Science and Industry (MOSI).** 4801 E. Fowler Ave. (at N. 50th St.). ☎ **813/987-6300** or 813/987-6100 for recorded information. www.mosi.org. Admission $13 adults; $11 seniors, college students with iden-tification, and children 13–18; $9 children 2–12; free for children under 2. Admission includes IMAX movies. Daily 9am–5pm or later. From downtown, take I-275 north, then Fowler Ave. east 2 miles to museum on right.

A great place to take the kids on a rainy day, MOSI is the largest science center in the Southeast and has more than 450 interactive exhibits. You can step into the Gulf Hurricane and experience 74 m.p.h. winds, defy the laws of gravity in the unique *Challenger* space experience, cruise the mysterious world of microbes in LifeLab, and explore the human body in The Amazing You. Our Florida focuses on the state's environment, and Our Place in the Universe will introduce you to space, flight, and beyond. You can also watch stunning movies in Florida's first IMAX dome theater. When you tire of being indoors, trails wind through a 47-acre nature preserve with a butterfly garden.

Tampa Museum of Art. 600 N. Ashley Dr. (at Twiggs St.), downtown. ☎ **813/274-8130.** www.tampamuseum.com. Admission $5 adults, $4 seniors, $3 students with identification and children 6–18, free for children 5 and under, by donation for everyone Thurs 5–8pm and Sat 10am–noon. Tues–Wed and Fri–Sat 10am–5pm, Thurs 10am–8pm, Sun 1–5pm. Parking 90¢ per hour. Take I-275 to Exit 25 (Ashley St.).

Located on the east bank of the Hillsborough River next to the round NationsBank building (locals facetiously call it the "Beer Can") and just south of the Tampa Bay Performing Arts Center, this fine-arts complex offers eight galleries with changing exhibits ranging from classical antiquities to contemporary Florida art. There's also a 7-acre riverfront park and sculpture garden.

VENTURING INTO YBOR CITY

Northeast of downtown, the city's historic Latin district takes its present name from Don Vicente Martinez Ybor ("*Ee*-bore," a Spanish cigar maker who arrived here in 1886 via Cuba and Key West. Soon his and other Tampa factories were producing more than 300,000 hand-rolled stogies a day.

It may not be the cigar capital of the world anymore, but Ybor is the happening part of Tampa, and it's one of the best places in Florida to buy hand-rolled cigars. It's not on a par with New Orleans's Bourbon Street, Washington's Georgetown, or New York's SoHo, but good food and great music dominate the scene, especially on weekends when the streets bustle until 4am. Live-music offerings run the gamut from jazz and blues to indie rock. At the heart of it all is **Centro Ybor,** a new dining-shopping-entertainment complex at 7th Avenue and 19th Street.

Even if you're not a cigar smoker, you'll enjoy a stroll through the **Ybor City State Museum,** 1818 9th Ave., between 18th and 19th streets (☎ **813/247-6323;** www.dep.state.fl.us/parks/District_4/YborCity/), housed in the former Ferlita Bakery (1896–1973). You can take a self-guided tour around the museum to see a collection of cigar labels, cigar memorabilia, and works by local artisans. Admission is $2 per person, including a 15-minute guided tour of **La Casita,** a renovated cigar worker's cottage adjacent to the museum; it's furnished as it was at the turn of the century. The museum is open daily from 9am to noon and 1 to 5pm, but plan to be here when La Casita is open, daily from 10am to noon and 1 to 2:30pm.

Check with the museum about **walking tours** of the historic district. **Ybor City Ghost Walks** (☎ **813/242-9255**) will take you to the spookier parts of the area at night. Call for reservations, schedules, and prices.

Housed in a 100-year-old, three-story former cigar factory, **Ybor City Brewing Company,** 2205 N. 20th St., facing Palm Avenue (☎ **813/242-9222**), produces Ybor Gold and other brews, none with preservatives. Admission of $2 per person includes a tour of the brewery and taste of the end result. Open Tuesday to Saturday from 11am to 3pm.

ORGANIZED TOURS

Swiss Chalet Tours, 3601 E. Busch Blvd. (☎ **813/985-3601**), opposite Busch Gardens in the privately run Tampa Bay Visitor

Information Center (see "Essentials," above), operates guided bus tours of Tampa, Ybor City, and environs. The 4-hour tours of Tampa are given from 10am to 2pm daily, with a stop for lunch at the Columbia Restaurant in Ybor City. They cost $40 for adults and $35 for children. The 7-hour full-day tours of both Tampa and St. Petersburg cost $70 for adults and $65 for children. Reservations are required at least 24 hours in advance; passengers are picked up at major hotels and various other points in the Tampa/St. Petersburg area. You also can book bus tours to Orlando, Sarasota, Bradenton, and other regional destinations (call for schedules, prices, and reservations).

4 Outdoor Pursuits & Spectator Sports

BIKING, IN-LINE SKATING & JOGGING

Bayshore Boulevard, a 7-mile promenade, is famous for its sidewalk right on the shores of Hillsborough Bay. Reputed to be the world's longest continuous sidewalk, it's a favorite for runners, joggers, walkers, and in-line skaters. The route goes from the western edge of downtown in a southward direction, passing stately old homes of Hyde Park, a few high-rise condos, retirement communities, and houses of worship, ending at Ballast Point Park. The view from the promenade across the bay to the downtown skyline is unmatched here (Bayshore Boulevard also is great for a drive).

FISHING

One of Florida's best guide services, ✪ **Light Tackle Fishing Expeditions,** 6105 Memorial Hwy., Suite 4 (☎ **800/972-1930** or 813/963-1930), offers private sportfishing trips for tarpon, redfish, cobia, trout, and snook. Trips cost $140 per person. Call for schedule and required reservations.

GOLF

Tampa has three municipal golf courses where you can play for about $30, a relative pittance when compared to the privately owned courses here and elsewhere in Florida. The **Babe Zaharias Municipal Golf Course,** 11412 Forest Hills Dr., north of Lowry Park (☎ **813/631-4374**), is an 18-hole, par-70 course with a pro shop, putting greens, and a driving range. It's the shortest of the municipal courses, but small greens and narrow fairways present ample challenges. Water presents obstacles on 12 of the 18 holes at **Rocky Point Municipal Golf Course,** 4151 Dana Shores Dr. (☎ 813/673-4316), located between the airport and the bay. It's a par-71 course with a pro shop, practice range, and putting greens. On the Hillsborough River in north Tampa, the **Rogers Park Municipal Golf Course,** 7910 N. 30th St. (☎ 813/673-4396), is an 18-hole, par-72 championship course with a lighted driving and practice range. They all are open daily from 7am to dusk, and lessons and club rentals are available.

Another inexpensive place to play is the **University of South Florida Golf Course,** Fletcher Avenue and 46th Street (☎ 813/632-6893), just north of the USF campus. This 18-hole, par-71 course is nicknamed "The Claw" because of its challenging layout. It offers lessons and club rentals. Greens fees range from about $19 to $25, or $25 to $35 with a cart, depending on the season and time of day. It's open daily from 7am to dusk.

Other public courses include the **Hall of Fame Golf Club,** just south of the airport at 2222 N. Westshore Blvd. (☎ 813/876-4913), an 18-hole, par-72 affair with a driving range; **Persimmon Hill Golf Club,** 5109 Hamey Rd. (☎ 813/623-6962); **Silver Dollar Trap & Golf Club,** 17000 Patterson Rd., Odessa (☎ 813/920-3884); and **Westchase Golf Club,** 1307 Radcliff Dr. (☎ 813/854-2331).

You can book starting times and get information about these and the area's other courses by calling **Tee Times USA** (☎ 800/374-8633).

If you want to do some serious work on your game, the **Arnold Palmer Golf Academy World Headquarters** is at Saddlebrook Resort, 5700 Saddlebrook Way, Wesley Chapel, 12 miles north of Tampa (☎ 800/729-8383 or 813/973-1111; www.saddlebrookresort.com). Half-day and hourly instruction is available, and there are 2-, 3-, and 5-day programs available for adults and juniors. You have to stay at the resort or enroll in the golf program to play at Saddlebrook. See "Where to Stay," below, for more information about the resort.

SPECTATOR SPORTS

National Football League fans can catch the defensive-minded **Tampa Bay Buccaneers** at the modern, 66,000-seat Raymond James Stadium, 4201 N. Dale Mabry Hwy., at Dr. Martin Luther King Jr. Boulevard (☎ 813/879-2827; www.buccaneers.com). The Bucs' season runs from September through December.

The National Hockey League's **Tampa Bay Lightning** play in the Ice Palace, beginning in October (☎ **813/229-8800;** www.tampabaylightning.com).

New York Yankees fans can watch the Boys in Blue during baseball spring training from mid-February through March at Legends Field (☎ **813/879-2244** or 813/875-7753; www. yankees.com), opposite Raymond James Stadium. A scaled-down replica of Yankee Stadium, it's the largest spring-training facility in Florida, with a 10,000-seat capacity. Tickets range from $6 to $10. Parking costs $6. The club's minor league team, the **Tampa Yankees** (same phone and Web site), plays at Legends Field from April through August.

The only oval thoroughbred race course on Florida's west coast, ✪ **Tampa Bay Downs,** 11225 Racetrack Rd., Oldsmar (☎ **800/200-4434** in Florida, or 813/855-4401), is the home of the Tampa Bay Derby. Races are held from December to May, and the track presents simulcasts year-round. Call for post times.

TENNIS
Beginners to highly skilled players can sharpen their games at the **Hopman Tennis Program,** at the Saddlebrook Resort, 5700 Saddlebrook Way, Wesley Chapel (☎ **800/729-8383** or 813/973-1111; www.saddlebrookresort.com). You must be a member or a guest to play here (see "Where to Stay," below).

5 Shopping

HYDE PARK
Old Hyde Park Village, 1507 W. Swann Ave., at South Dakota Avenue (☎ **813/251-3500**), is a terrific alternative to cookie-cutter suburban malls. Walk around little shops in the sunshine and check out Hyde Park, one of the city's oldest and most historic neighborhoods at the same time. The cluster of 50 upscale shops and boutiques is set in a village layout. The selection includes Williams-Sonoma, Pottery Barn, Banana Republic, Brooks Brothers, Crabtree & Evelyn, Godiva Chocolatier, Polo Ralph Lauren, and Talbots, to name a few. There's a free parking garage on South Oregon Avenue behind Jacobson's department store. The shops are open Monday to Wednesday and Saturday from 10am to 6pm, Thursday and Friday from 10am to 9pm, and Sunday from noon to 5pm.

HAND-ROLLED CIGARS

Ybor City no longer is a major producer of hand-rolled cigars, but you can watch artisans making stogies at the **Gonzales y Martinez Cigar Factory,** 2025 7th Ave., in the Columbia Restaurant building (☎ **813/247-2469**). Gonzales and Martinez are recent arrivals from Cuba and don't speak English, but the staff does at the adjoining **Columbia Cigar Store** (it's best to enter here). Rollers are on duty Monday to Saturday from 10am to 6pm.

You can stock up on fine domestic and imported cigars at **El Sol,** 1728 E. 7th Ave. (☎ **813/247-5554**), the city's oldest cigar store; **King Corona Cigar Factory,** 1523 E. 7th Ave. (☎ **813/241-9109**); and at **Metropolitan Cigars & Wine,** 2014 E. 7th Ave. (☎ **813/248-3304**).

MALLS

The main mall in the city is **West Shore Plaza,** on Kennedy Boulevard where it turns into Memorial Highway (Fla. 60). **University Mall** is nearest Busch Gardens, on Fowler Avenue just east of I-275. The area's largest complex is **Brandon TownCenter,** at I-4 and Fla. 60 in the eastern suburb of Brandon, where most stores have unusually large amounts of floor space and, hence, more merchandise from which to choose.

6 Where to Stay

I've organized the accommodations listings below into three geographic areas: near Busch Gardens, downtown, and Ybor City. If you're going to Busch Gardens, Adventure Island, Lowry Park Zoo, and the Museum of Science and Industry (MOSI), the motels near Busch Gardens are much more convenient than those downtown, about 7 miles to the south. The downtown hotels are geared to business travelers, but staying there will put you near the Florida Aquarium, the Tampa Museum of Art, the Henry B. Plant Museum, the Tampa Bay Performing Arts Center, scenic Bayshore Boulevard, and the dining and shopping opportunities in the Hyde Park historic district, and Ybor City's restaurants and nightlife. Or you can avoid driving to Ybor City and stay at Hilton's new hotel just 2 blocks from the action.

The Westshore area, near the bay west of downtown and south of Tampa International Airport, is another commercial center,

Tampa Accommodations & Dining

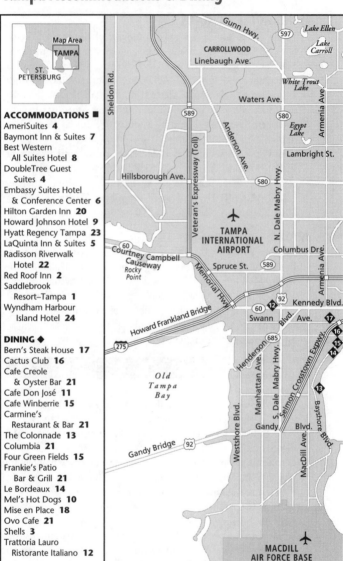

Map Area
TAMPA
ST. PETERSBURG

ACCOMMODATIONS ■
AmeriSuites **4**
Baymont Inn & Suites **7**
Best Western
  All Suites Hotel **8**
DoubleTree Guest
  Suites **4**
Embassy Suites Hotel
  & Conference Center **6**
Hilton Garden Inn **20**
Howard Johnson Hotel **9**
Hyatt Regency Tampa **23**
LaQuinta Inn & Suites **5**
Radisson Riverwalk
  Hotel **22**
Red Roof Inn **2**
Saddlebrook
  Resort–Tampa **1**
Wyndham Harbour
  Island Hotel **24**

DINING ◆
Bern's Steak House **17**
Cactus Club **16**
Cafe Creole
  & Oyster Bar **21**
Cafe Don José **11**
Cafe Winberrie **15**
Carmine's
  Restaurant & Bar **21**
The Colonnade **13**
Columbia **21**
Four Green Fields **15**
Frankie's Patio
  Bar & Grill **21**
Le Bordeaux **14**
Mel's Hot Dogs **10**
Mise en Place **18**
Ovo Cafe **21**
Shells **3**
Trattoria Lauro
  Ristorante Italiano **12**

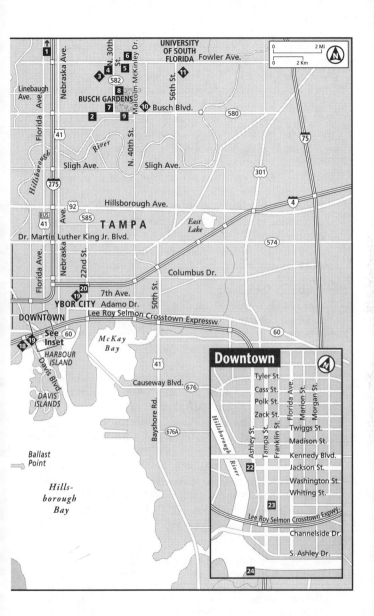

with a wide range of national chain hotels catering to business travelers and conventioneers. It's convenient to Raymond James Stadium and the New York Yankees' spring training complex. Check with your favorite chain for a Westshore Airport location.

The high season in Tampa generally runs from January to April, but you won't find as large an increase here as at the beach resorts. Most hotels offer discounted package rates in the summer and weekend specials all year, dropping their rates by as much as 50%. Hotels often combine tickets to major attractions like Busch Gardens in their packages, so always ask about special deals.

Hillsborough River State Park, 15402 U.S. 301 North, Thonotosassa, FL 33592 (☎ **813/986-1020;** www.dep.state. fl.us/parks/District_4/HillsboroughRiver/), offers 118 campsites year-round, plus fishing, canoeing, and boating.

Hillsborough County adds 12% tax to your hotel room bill.

NEAR BUSCH GARDENS

The nearest chain motel to the park is **Howard Johnson Hotel Near Busch Gardens Maingate,** 4139 E. Busch Blvd. (☎ **800/ 444-5656** or 813/988-9191), an older property that was extensively renovated and reopened in 1999. It's 1¹/₂ blocks east of the main entrance.

A bit farther away, the 500-room **Embassy Suites Hotel and Conference Center,** 3705 Spectrum Blvd., actually facing Fowler Avenue (☎ **800/EMBASSY** or 813/977-7066; fax 977-7933), is the plushest and most expensive establishment near the park. Almost across the avenue stands **LaQuinta Inn & Suites,** 3701 E. Fowler Ave. (☎ **800/NU-ROOMS** or 813/910-7500; fax 813/910-7600). Side-by-side just south of Fowler Avenue are editions of **AmeriSuites,** 11408 N. 30th St. (☎ **800/833-1516** or 813/979-1922; fax 813/979-1926), and **DoubleTree Guest Suites,** 11310 N. 30th St. (☎ **800/ 222-TREE** or 813/971-7690; fax 813/972-5525).

MODERATE

✪ **Best Western All Suites Hotel Near USF Behind Busch Gardens.** 3001 University Center Dr. (faces N. 30th St. between Busch Blvd. and Flower Ave.), Tampa, FL 33612. ☎ **800/786-7446** or 813/971-8930. Fax 813/971-8935. www.thatparrotplace.com. 150 units. A/C TV TEL. Winter $99–$159 suite for 2. Off-season $89–$139 suite for 2. Rates include full breakfast buffet and evening beer-and-wine reception. AE, DC, DISC, MC, V.

About 1 mile from the Busch Gardens entrance, this 3-story hacienda-style building is the most beachlike vacation venue you'll find close to the park. Whimsical signs will lead you around a lush tropical courtyard with heated pool, hot tub, covered games area, sun deck (with data ports in the surrounding railing), and a lively, sports-oriented tiki bar known as Ruzic's Roost (in honor of hands-on owner John Ruzic). The bar can get noisy before closing at 9pm, and bare-footed, wet-bathing-suited guests can leave some of the ground-level units musty, so ask for an upstairs suite away from the action.

The suites' living rooms have sofa beds, La-Z-Boy recliners, dining tables, wet bars, microwaves, phones, TVs, VCRs, and stereo units. Their separate bedrooms are equipped with TVs, phones, built-in armoire and mirrored vanity areas, and narrow screened patios or balconies. Great for kids, 11 "family suites" have over-and-under bunk beds in addition to a queen-size bed for parents. Another 28 suites are especially equipped for business travelers, with ergonomic chairs at big writing desks with speakerphones.

Guests can graze a complimentary breakfast buffet, and the tiki bar serves inexpensive chargrilled ribs, burgers, fish, and chicken for dinner. Happy hour between 4 and 6pm features 99¢–draft beers, wine, and some mixed drinks—a good deal for both guests and local residents. Facilities also include a 24-hour gift shop/food store, videotape rentals, whirlpool, meeting rooms, and coin-operated laundry. Sports teams visiting the nearby University of South Florida like to stay here.

Baymont Inn & Suites. 9202 N. 30th St. (at Busch Blvd.), Tampa, FL 33612. ☎ **800/428-3438** or 813/930-6900. Fax 813/930-0563. www.baymontinns. com. 146 units. A/C TV TEL. Winter $80–$85 double. Off-season $65–$85 double. Rates include continental breakfast. AE, DC, DISC, MC, V.

Fake banana trees and a parrot cage welcome guests to the terra-cotta-floored lobby of this comfortable and convenient member of the former Budgetel Inn chain of cost-conscious but amenity-rich motels. All rooms are spacious and have ceiling fans, bright wood furniture with tropical trim, desks, and phones with long cords. Rooms with king beds also have recliners. Outside, a courtyard with an unheated swimming pool has plenty of space for sunning. There's a game room and coin laundry, and local telephone calls are free. There's no restaurant on the premises, but plenty are nearby.

INEXPENSIVE

Red Roof Inn. 2307 E. Busch Blvd. (between 22nd and 26th sts.), Tampa, FL 33612. ☎ **800/THE-ROOF** or 813/932-0073. Fax 813/933-5689. 108 units. A/C TV TEL. Winter $59 single or double. Off-season $49 single or double. AE, DC, DISC, MC, V.

Less than a mile from Busch Gardens, this is the best low-budget choice here. Most of the rooms in the pleasant, 2-story building are away from the road, as are an outdoor swimming pool and whirlpool, both in a landscaped setting. Most of the clean, well-maintained rooms are done up in bright colors. Free local phone calls.

DOWNTOWN TAMPA

✪ **Hyatt Regency Tampa.** 2 Tampa City Center (corner of Tampa and E. Jackson sts.), Tampa, FL 33602. ☎ **800/233-1234** or 813/225-1234. Fax 813/273-0234. 521 units. A/C TV TEL. $99–$270 double. Weekend packages available in summer. AE, DC, DISC, MC, V. Valet parking $7.

In the center of the downtown business district, it's not surprising that this Hyatt—thoroughly renovated to the tune of $11 million in 1998–1999—caters primarily to the corporate crowd. It's just off the Franklin Street pedestrian mall. The Hyatt signature eight-story atrium lobby has a cascading waterfall and lots of foliage. The City Center Cafe serves breakfast and lunch, while Avanzare provides inexpensive light lunches (office workers congregate), moderately priced dinners, and a lounge with libations and piano music (there's not much else going in downtown after dark). Amenities include concierge, 24-hour room service, newspaper delivery, child care, business center, valet laundry, guest laundry, airport courtesy shuttle, outdoor heated swimming pool, whirlpool, and exercise room.

Radisson Riverwalk Hotel. 200 N. Ashley St. (at Jackson St.), Tampa, FL 33602. ☎ **800/333-3333** or 813/233-2222. Fax 813/221-5929. 284 units. A/C TV TEL. Winter $159 double. Off-season $99–$119. AE DC, DISC, MC, V. Valet parking $5.

Sitting on the east bank of the Hillsborough River, this six-story was completely remodeled in 1998. Half the rooms face west and have views from their balconies of the Arabesque minarets atop the Henry B. Plant Museum across the river—quite a scene at sunset. They cost the same as units on the east, which face downtown's skyscrapers, so be sure to request a riverside room. Sporting quality Drexel Heritage furniture, the spacious rooms have coffeemakers, hair dryers, phones with data ports, and either two full beds or a king bed and writing desk. Beside the river, the Ashley Street Grill serves indoor-outdoor breakfasts and lunches, then turns to fine dining in the evenings. Open from 5am to 1am, Boulanger baker and deli purveys fresh pastries, soups, sandwiches, and snacks. A brick deck surrounds the outdoor riverside pool with its own bar. Amenities include concierge and valet laundry service.

✪ **Wyndham Harbour Island Hotel.** 725 S. Harbour Island Blvd., Harbour Island, Tampa, FL 33602. ☎ **800/WYNDHAM** or 813/229-5000. Fax 813/229-5322. 299 units. A/C MINIBAR TV TEL. Winter $149–$229 double. Off-season $109–$209 double. Valet parking $8, self-parking $6. AE, DC, DISC, MC, V.

There's not much action on Harbour Island, a troubled urban development project that never found tenants for its waterfront shopping-and-dining complex, but you'll enjoy quiet elegance at this 12-story hotel, the downtown area's most luxurious digs. All with water views, the bedrooms here are plushly furnished in dark woods and floral fabrics, and each has a well-lit marble-trimmed bathroom, executive desk, and work area. Watch the yachts drift by as you dine at the Harbourview Room, or enjoy your favorite drink in the Bar, a clubby room with equally good views. Snacks and drinks are available during the day at the Pool Bar. Amenities here include concierge, limited room service, secretarial services, notary public, evening turndown, valet laundry, courtesy airport shuttle, outdoor heated swimming pool with adjacent bar, newsstand/gift shop, guest privileges at nearby health club.

Note: Before staying here, inquire if the on-again, off-again People Mover is operating (see "Getting Around," above). If it is, then it's a 1-minute tram ride above Garrison Channel to downtown. Otherwise, you'll have to take roundabout route to the business district.

YBOR CITY

Hilton Garden Inn. 1700 E. 9th Ave. (between 17th and 18th sts.), Tampa, FL 33605. ☎ **800/HILTONS** or 813/769-9267. Fax 813/769-3299. 95 units. A/C TV TEL. $89–$189 double. AE, DC, DISC, MC, V.

Built in 1999, this four-story hotel stands just 2 blocks north of the heart of Ybor City's dining and entertainment district. A one-story structure in front houses the bright lobby, a comfy relaxation area with fireplace, a restaurant providing cooked and continental breakfasts, and a small pantry selling beer, wine, soft drinks, and frozen dinners. You can heat up the dinners in your comfortable guest room's microwave oven or store them your fridge. Since Hilton's "Garden" hotels are aimed primarily at business travelers (they compete with Marriott's Courtyards), your room also will have a large desk and two phones with data ports. If you opt for a suite, you'll have a separate living room and a larger bathroom than in the regular units. You can pump iron in a small exercise room, swim in a heated outdoor pool, or soak in the adjacent whirlpool. Other amenities include newspaper delivery and a business center.

A NEARBY RESORT

✪ **Saddlebrook Resort-Tampa.** 5700 Saddlebrook Way, Wesley Chapel, FL 33543. ☎ **800/729-8383** or 813/973-1111. Fax 813/973-4504. www. saddlebrookresort.com. E-mail: info@saddlebrookresort.com. 800 units. A/C TV TEL. Winter $185–$197 per person. Off-season $120–$132 per person. Rates include breakfast and dinner. Packages available. AE, DC, DISC, MC, V. Valet parking $3; free self-parking. Take I-75 north to Fla. 54 (Exit 58), go 1 mile east to resort.

Set on 480 rolling acres, this spa and golf and tennis resort is off the beaten path (30 minutes north of Tampa International Airport) but worth the trip. You can treat yourself to complete spa treatments, join the pros at the Hopman Tennis Program, or perfect your swing at the Arnold Palmer Golf Academy (see "Outdoor Activities & Spectator Sports," above). This is a condo development, so you'll stay in privately owned hotel rooms or one-, two-, or three-bedroom suites. Much more appealing than the rooms, the suites have kitchens and a patio or balcony over looking lagoons, cypress and palm trees, and the resort's two 18-hole championship golf courses.

Dining/Diversions: The casual but elegant Cypress Restaurant consistently wins accolades for its Florida seafood. Enjoy beef in Dempsey's Steakhouse or catch a game at the adjacent TD's Sports Bar. The Poolside Cafe is great for alfresco dining in your bathing suit. The Polo Lounge provides music for dancing nightly.

Amenities: Concierge, valet parking, limited room service, newspaper delivery, in-room massage, child care, children's activities program, airport courtesy shuttle, business center, 36 holes of golf, 45 tennis courts, 270-foot-long half-million-gallon Superpool, whirlpool, 7,000-square-foot luxury spa, fitness center, basketball and volleyball courts, softball field.

7 Where to Dine

As with the hotels, I have organized the restaurants below by geographic area: near Busch Gardens, in or near Hyde Park (just across the Hillsborough River from downtown), and in Ybor City (on the northeastern edge of downtown).

NEAR BUSCH GARDENS

You'll find the national fast food and family restaurants east of I-275 on Busch Boulevard and along Fowler Avenue near University Mall.

Cafe Don José. 11009 N. 56th St. (in Sherwood Forest Shopping Center, $^1/_4$-mile south of Fowler Ave.). ☎ **813/985-2392.** Main courses $13–$20. AE, DC, MC, V. Tues–Fri 11:30am–4:30pm and 5–10pm, Sat 5–10pm. SPANISH/AMERICAN.

It's not nearly on par with Columbia in Ybor City (see below), but this Spanish-themed restaurant is the best there is within a short drive ($2^1/_2$ miles) of Busch Gardens. High-back chairs, dark wood floors, and Spanish posters and paintings set an appropriate scene for the house specialties, traditional paella and Valencia-style rice dishes (allow 30 minutes preparation time for each). Don José also offers non-Spanish fare such as chateaubriand and red snapper baked in parchment. Burgers join many of the dinner main courses—at half price—on the lunch menu.

Mel's Hot Dogs. 4136 E. Busch Blvd., at 42nd St. ☎ **813/985-8000.** Reservations not accepted. Hot dogs, burgers, sandwiches $2–$6.50. No credit cards. Daily 11am–9pm. AMERICAN.

Catering to everyone from businesspeople on a lunch break to hungry families craving inexpensive all-beef hot dogs, this red-and-white cottage offers everything from "bagel dogs" and corn dogs to a bacon/cheddar Reuben. All choices are served on a poppy seed bun and most come with french fries and a choice of coleslaw or baked beans. Even the decor is dedicated to wieners: The walls and windows are lined with hot-dog memorabilia. And just in case hot dog mania hasn't won you over, there are a few alternative choices (sausages, chicken breast, beef and veggie burgers, and terrific onion rings).

Shells. 11010 N. 30th St. (between Busch Blvd. and Fowler Ave.). ☎ **813/977-8456.** Reservations not accepted. Main courses $6–$17 (most $8.50–$11). AE, DISC, MC, V. Sun–Thurs 11:30am–10pm, Fri–Sat 11:30am–11pm. SEAFOOD.

You'll see Shells restaurants in many parts of Florida, and with good reason, for this casual, award-winning chain consistently provides excellent value, especially if you have a family to feed (there's a children's menu). They all have virtually identical menus, prices, and hours. Particularly good are the spicy Jack Daniel's buffalo shrimp and scallop appetizers. Main courses range from the usual fried seafood platters to pastas and charcoal-grilled shrimp, fish, steaks, and chicken. Much of the seafood here has been frozen, so you're better off ordering it fried or with sauces. I counted 21 tender, bite-size shrimp in a light, garlic-tinged cream sauce and served over linguine—a bargain for less than $10.

HYDE PARK
EXPENSIVE

Bern's Steak House. 1208 S. Howard Ave. (at Marjory Ave.). ☎ **813/251-2421.** Reservations required. Main courses $20–$36. AE, DC, DISC, MC, V. Daily 5–11pm. Closed Christmas. AMERICAN.

The exterior of this famous steak house looks like a factory built almost under the Lee Roy Selmon Crosstown Expressway. Inside, however, you'll find eight ornate dining rooms with themes like Rhône, Burgundy, and Irish Rebellion. Their dark atmospheres are perfect for meat lovers, for here you order and pay for charcoal-grilled steaks (beef or buffalo) according to the thickness and weight (a 60-ounce, 3-inch-thick Porterhouse can run up to $168). They come with onion soup, salad, baked potato, garlic toast, onion rings, and vegetables grown in Bern's own organic garden. The phone book–size wine list offers more than 7,000 selections.

The big surprise here is the dessert quarters upstairs, where 50 romantic booths paneled in aged California redwood can privately seat from 2 to 12 guests. Each of these little chambers is equipped with a phone for placing your order and a closed-circuit TV for watching and listening to a resident pianist. The dessert menu offers almost 100 delicious selections, plus some 1,400 after-dinner drinks. It's possible to reserve a booth for dessert only, but preference is given to those who dine.

Le Bordeaux. 1502 S. Howard Ave. (2 blocks north of Bayshore Blvd.). ☎ **813/254-4387.** Reservations recommended. Main courses $16–$32. AE, DC, MC, V. Mon–Sat 5:30–10pm, Sun 5–9pm. CLASSICAL FRENCH.

This bistro's authentic French fare is some of the region's best, but keep a reign on your credit card—everything's sold à la carte, so you can ring up a hefty bill quickly. French-born chef/owner Gordon Davis offers seating in a living room–style main dining room of this converted house expanded to include a plant-filled conservatory. His classical French menu changes monthly, but you can count on homemade pâtés and pastries, and specials such as *filet de snook a la pistache* (local snook encrusted with pistachio nuts). Part of the establishment is the lounge-style Left Bank Jazz Bistro, with live entertainment Thursday to Saturday from 9pm.

MODERATE

✪ **Mise en Place.** In Grand Central Place, 442 W. Kennedy Blvd. (at S. Magnolia Ave., opposite the University of Tampa). ☎ 813/254-5373. Reservations recommended. Main courses $15–$24; tasting menu $35. AE, DC, DISC, MC, V. Mon–Fri 11am–3pm, Tues–Thurs 5:30–10pm, Fri–Sat 5:30–11pm. ECLECTIC.

Look around at all those happy, stylish people soaking up the trendy ambience, and you'll know why chef Marty Blitz and his wife, Marianne, are among the culinary darlings of Tampa. They present the freshest of ingredients, with a creative menu that changes daily. Main courses often include fascinating-to-the-taste choices such as Creole-style mahimahi served with chili cheese grits and a ragout of black-eye peas, andouille sausage, and rock shrimp. There's dinnertime valet parking at the rear of the building on Grand Central Place, and you can walk here for lunch before or after touring the nearby Henry B. Plant Museum. There's live music in the lounge on Saturday from 9:30pm to 2am.

✪ **Trattoria Lauro Ristorante Italiano.** 3915 Henderson Blvd. (2 blocks west of Dale Mabry Hwy., between Watrous and Neptune Aves.). ☎ 813/281-2100. Reservations recommended. Main courses $10–$20. AE, DC, DISC, MC, V. Mon–Fri 11:30am–2pm and 5:30–10pm, Sat 5:30–11pm, Sun 5:30–10pm. ITALIAN.

Known for extraordinary sauces and pastas, chef/owner Lauro Medeglia is a native Italian who cooks his home fare with love. Though his restaurant is off the beaten track, it's worth the detour. Classical decor and soft music have made it one of Tampa's favorite places to "pop the question," and smartly attired waiters render efficient yet friendly and unobtrusive service. Try the caprese, putanesca, gnocchi, or agnolotti.

INEXPENSIVE

✪ **Cactus Club.** In Old Hyde Park shopping complex, 1601 Snow Ave. (south of Swan St.). ☎ **813/251-4089.** Reservations not accepted. Burgers and sandwiches $7–$8; main courses $6.50–14. AE, DC, MC, V. Mon–Thurs 11am–11pm, Fri–Sat 11am–midnight, Sun 11am–10:30pm. AMERICAN SOUTHWEST.

You can definitely taste the freshness at this Texas roadhouse-style cantina in the middle of the Old Hyde Park shops, for all ingredients except the beans come straight from the market. My favorite dish is the "fundido"—a spicy casserole of marinated fajita-style chicken strips and sauteed vegetables topped with melted jack cheese, with beans and rice on the side. Other offerings are more traditional: tacos, enchiladas, chili, sizzling fajitas, hickory-smoked baby back ribs, Jamaican jerk chicken, burgers, quesadillas, enchiladas (including vegetarian versions), sandwiches, and smoked chicken salad. The lively Cactus Cantina bar is a favorite neighborhood watering hole. Dine inside or outside, but get here early at lunch time—it's usually packed.

Cafe Winberie. In Old Hyde Park shopping complex, 1610 Swann Ave. (at S. Dakota St.). ☎ **813/253-6500.** Reservations not accepted. Burgers and sandwiches $7–$10; main courses $6–$17. AE, DC, DISC, MC, V. Mon–Thurs 11am–11pm, Fri–Sat 11am–midnight. Sun 11am–10:30pm. INTERNATIONAL.

With both indoor and sidewalk seating, this Parisian-style bistro at Hyde Park's main intersection makes a fine retreat on your shopping excursion for a cold latte, a snack, or a full meal. Inside, cafe curtains, dark paneling, posters, and an antique wine rack behind the bar create a chic ambience. Start with bruschetta or cheese-filled portobello mushrooms, then proceed to consistently fine salmon roasted in parchment with fresh vegetables, or chicken breast sauteed in Marsala wine. Several pastas include shrimp and linguini tossed with basil, garlic, and tomatoes. Chocolate mousse is one of several delicious desserts.

The Colonnade. 3401 Bayshore Blvd. (at W. Julia St.). ☎ **813/839-7558.** Reservations accepted only for large parties. Main courses $8–$20 (most $11–15). AE, DC, DISC, MC, V. Sun–Thurs 11am–10pm, Fri–Sat 11am–11pm. SEAFOOD.

Local couples and families have been flocking to this rough-hewn, shiplap place since 1935, primarily for the great view of Hillsborough Bay across Bayshore Boulevard. The food is a bit on the Red Lobster-ish side, but the vista from the window tables more than makes up for any shortcomings in the fresh seafood:

grouper prepared seven ways, crab-stuffed flounder, Maryland-style crab cakes, even wild Florida alligator as an appetizer. Prime rib, steaks, and chicken are also available.

Four Green Fields. 205 W. Platt St. (between Parker St. and Plant Ave.). ☎ **813/254-4444.** Reservations accepted. Sandwiches $6; main courses $8.50–$14. AE, MC, V. Daily 11am–3am. IRISH/AMERICAN.

Just across the bridge from the downtown convention center, America's only thatched-roof Irish pub may be surrounded by palm trees instead of potato fields, but it still offers the ambience and tastes of Ireland. Staffed by genuine Irish immigrants, the large room with a square bar in the center smells of Irish ale. The Gaelic stew is predictably bland, but the salads and sandwiches are passable. The crowd usually is young, especially for live Irish music on Thursday, Friday, and Saturday nights.

YBOR CITY
MODERATE

○ **Cafe Creole and Oyster Bar.** 1330 9th Ave. (at Avenida de Republica de Cuba/14th St.). ☎ **813/247-6283.** Reservations not accepted but call for preferred seating. Main courses $9.50–$19. AE, DC, DISC, MC, V. Mon–Thurs 11:30am–10pm, Fri 11:30am–11:30pm, Sat 5–11:30pm. CREOLE/CAJUN.

Resembling a turn-of-the-century railway station, this brick building dates from 1896 and was originally known as El Pasaje, the home of the Cherokee Club, a gentlemen's hotel and private club with a casino and an opulent decor with stained-glass windows, wrought-iron balconies, Spanish murals, and marble bathrooms. Specialties include exceptionally prepared Louisiana crab cakes, oysters, blackened grouper, and jambalaya. If you're new to bayou cuisine, try the Creole sampler. Dine inside or out.

○ **Columbia.** 2117 E. 7th Ave. (between 21st and 22nd sts). ☎ **813/248-4961.** Reservations recommended. Main courses $12–$23. AE, DC, DISC, MC, V. Mon–Thurs 11am–10pm, Fri–Sat 11am–11pm, Sun noon–9pm. SPANISH.

Dating from 1905, this hand-painted tile building occupies an entire city block in the heart of Ybor City. Tourists flock here to soak up the ambience and so do the locals because it's so much fun to clap along during fire-belching Spanish flamenco floor shows in the main dining room. You can't help coming back time after time for the famous Spanish bean soup and original "1905" salad. The paella à la valenciana is outstanding, with more than a dozen ingredients from gulf grouper and gulf pink shrimp to calamari, mussels, clams, chicken, and pork. The decor throughout is graced with hand-painted tiles, wrought-iron chandeliers, dark woods, rich red fabrics, and stained-glass windows. You can breathe your own fumes in the Cigar Bar.

Frankie's Patio Bar & Grill. 1905 E. 7th Ave. (between 19th and 20th sts.). ☎ 813/249-3337. Reservations accepted only for large parties. Main courses $10–$15; sandwiches $5–$8. AE, DISC, MC, V. Mon–Tues 11am–3pm, Wed 11am–midnight, Thurs–Fri 11am–3am, Sat 5pm–3am. INTERNATIONAL.

This Ybor City attraction is known mostly as a venue for outstanding musical acts—live jazz, blues, reggae, and rock Wednesday to Saturday. With exposed industrial pipes, the large three-story restaurant stands out from the usual Spanish-themed, 19th-century architecture of Ybor City. There's seating indoors, on a large outdoor patio, or on an open-air balcony overlooking the street action. It's a fun atmosphere, and the food blends Cuban, American, Creole, and Italian influences. Build-your-own sandwiches are available during all hours.

INEXPENSIVE

✪ **Carmine's Restaurant & Bar.** 1802 E. 7th Ave. (at 18th St.) ☎ 813/248-3834. Reservations not accepted. Sandwiches $4–$8; main courses $7–$15. No credit cards. Mon–Tues 11am–10pm, Wed–Thurs 11am–midnight, Fri–Sat 11am–3am, Sun 11am–6pm. CUBAN/ITALIAN/AMERICAN.

Bright blue poles hold up an ancient pressed-tin ceiling above this noisy corner cafe, one of Ybor's most popular hangouts. A great variety of loyal local patrons gather here for genuine Cuban sandwiches—smoked ham, roast pork, Genoa salami, Swiss cheese, pickles, salad dressing, mustard, lettuce, and tomato on a crispy, submarine roll. There's a vegetarian version, too, and a combination half sandwich and choice of black beans and rice or a bowl of Spanish soup made with sausages, potatoes, and garbanzo beans—all make a hearty meal for just $4. Main courses are led by Cuban-style roast pork, thin-cut pork chops with mushroom sauce, spaghetti with a blue crab tomato sauce, and a few seafood and chicken platters.

Ovo Cafe. 1901 E. 7th Ave. (at 19th St.). ☎ 813/248-6979. Reservations strongly recommended Fri–Sat. Main courses $6.50–$13.50. AE, DC, DISC, MC, V. Mon–Tues 11am–3pm, Wed–Thurs 11am–10am, Fri–Sat 11am–2am, Sun 11am–9pm. INTERNATIONAL.

This cafe, popular with the business set by day and the club crowd on weekend nights, features a melange of sophisticated offerings. Pierogies and pasta pillows come with taste-tempting sauces and fillings. The likes of tangy jerk sauce over chicken, bananas, mozzarella cheese, and roasted sweet peppers top the individual-size pizzas. Strawberries or blackberries and a splash of liqueur cover the thick waffles. And there are several creative salads. Portions are substantial, but be careful with your credit card here: pricing is strictly à la carte. The big black bar dispenses a wide variety of Martinis, plus some unusual liqueur drinks.

8 Tampa After Dark

The Tampa/Hillsborough Arts Council maintains an **Artsline** (☎ **813/229-ARTS**), a 24-hour information service providing the latest on current and upcoming cultural events. Racks in many restaurants and bars have copies of *Weekly Planet, Focus,* and *Accent on Tampa Bay,* three free publications detailing what's going on in the entire bay area. And you can check the "Baylife" and "Friday Extra" sections of the *Tampa Tribune* and the Friday "Weekend" section of the *St. Petersburg Times.* The visitors center usually has copies of the week's newspaper sections (see "Essentials," above).

THE CLUB & MUSIC SCENE

Ybor City is Tampa's favorite nighttime venue by far. All you have to do is stroll along 7th Avenue East between 15th and 20th streets and you'll hear music blaring out of the clubs. The avenue is packed with people, a majority of them high-schoolers and early twenty-somethings, on Friday and Saturday from 9pm to 3am, but you'll also find something going on from Tuesday to Thursday and even on Sunday. You don't need addresses or phone numbers; your ears will guide you along 7th Avenue East.

Parking can be scarce during nighttime here, and the area has seen an occasional robbery late at night, so play it safe and use the municipal parking lots behind the shops on 8th Avenue East.

Starting at 15th Street and heading east, you'll come first to **The Masquerade,** with retro and old wave bands on Friday to Sunday. The body-pierced 20-something crowd gets primed at **Club Hedo, Atomic Age Cafe & Lounge,** and **Cherry's** before dancing at **The Rubb** across the avenue.

At 16th Street you will come to **Centro Ybor,** a dining, shopping, and entertainment complex that was scheduled to come on line in 2000.

Between 17th and 18th streets, you'll smell the cigar smoke coming from the sidewalk tables of the **Green Iguana Bar & Grill,** a refined establishment frequented by young professionals. The **Irish Pub** is just that, while **Fat Tuesday** has a large dance floor and long bar. Between 18th and 19th streets, you'll see **Harpo's,** which doesn't extract a cover charge. Keep going across 19th Street to one of Ybor's best clubs, **Blues Ship Café on Top,** which features live blues, jazz, and reggae. And last but not least is the warehouselike **Frankie's Patio Bar & Grill,** known for its reasonably priced food as well as its outstanding musical acts (see "Where to Dine," above). Across the avenue, country meets city at **Spurs in Ybor,** a country-and-western joint.

Elsewhere in town, you can lose your life savings playing bingo, poker, and the video slot machines at the **Seminole Indian Casino,** 5223 N. Orient Rd., at Hillsborough Road east of the city (☎ **800/282-7016** or 813/621-1302). It's open 24 hours every day of the year.

THE PERFORMING ARTS

With a prime downtown location on 9 acres along the east bank of the Hillsborough River, the huge ✪ **Tampa Bay Performing Arts Center,** 1010 N. MacInnes Place (☎ **800/955-1045** or 813/229-STAR), is the largest performing-arts venue south of the Kennedy Center in Washington, D.C. Accordingly, this four-theater complex is the focal point of Tampa's performing arts scene, presenting a wide range of Broadway plays, classical and pop concerts, operas, cabarets, improv, and special events.

A sightseeing attraction in its own right, the restored ✪ **Tampa Theatre,** 711 Franklin St. (☎ **813/223-8981**), between Zack and Polk streets, dates from 1926 and is on the National Register of Historic Places. It presents a varied program of classic, foreign, and alternative films, as well as concerts and special events.

The 66,321-seat **Raymond James Stadium,** 4201 N. Dale Mabry Hwy. (☎ **813/673-4300**), is frequently the site of headliner concerts. The **USF Sun Dome,** 4202 E. Fowler Ave. (☎ **813/974-3111**), on the University of South Florida campus, hosts major concerts by touring pop stars, rock bands, jazz groups, and other contemporary artists.

TicketMaster (☎ **813/287-8844**) sells tickets to most events and shows.

St. Petersburg

On the western shore of the bay, St. Petersburg stands in contrast to Tampa, much like San Francisco compares to Oakland in California. While Tampa is the area's business, industrial, and shipping center, St. Petersburg was conceived and built almost a century ago primarily for tourists and wintering snowbirds. Here you'll find one of the most picturesque and pleasant downtowns of any city in Florida, with a waterfront promenade and the famous, pyramid-shaped Pier offering great views across the bay, plus quality museums, interesting shops, and fine restaurants.

Away from downtown, the city pretty much consists of strip malls dividing residential neighborhoods, but plan at least to have a look around the charming bay-front area. If you don't do anything else, go out on The Pier and take a pleasant stroll along Bayshore Drive.

1 Orientation

ARRIVING

Tampa International Airport, approximately 16 miles northeast of St. Petersburg, is the prime gateway for the area (see "Getting There & Getting Around" in chapter 1). **St. Petersburg–Clearwater International Airport,** on Roosevelt Boulevard (Fla. 686) is about 10 miles north of downtown St. Petersburg (☎ **727/535-7600**).

It primarily handles charter flights by the Canadian carriers **Air Transat** (☎ **800/470-1011**) and **Canada 3000** (☎ **800/993-4378**), which fly here during the winter season. Limited regular service is provided by **American Trans Air** (☎ **800/225-2995**).

Alamo (☎ 800/327-9633), **Avis** (☎ 800/331-1212), **Budget** (☎ 800/527-0700), **Dollar** (☎ 800/800-4000), **Enterprise** (☎ 800/325-8007), **Hertz** (☎ 800/654-3131), and **National** (☎ 800/CAR-RENT) have rental-car operations here.

Downtown St. Petersburg

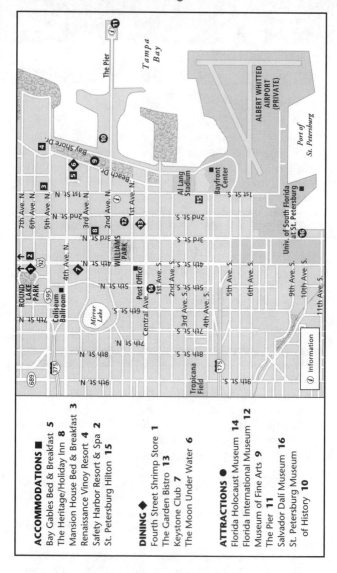

ACCOMMODATIONS ■

Bay Gables Bed & Breakfast **5**
The Heritage/Holiday Inn **8**
Mansion House Bed & Breakfast **3**
Renaissance Vinoy Resort **4**
Safety Harbor Resort & Spa **2**
St. Petersburg Hilton **15**

DINING ◆

Fourth Street Shrimp Store **1**
The Garden Bistro **13**
Keystone Club **7**
The Moon Under Water **6**

ATTRACTIONS ●

Florida Holocaust Museum **14**
Florida International Museum **12**
Museum of Fine Arts **9**
The Pier **11**
Salvador Dalí Museum **16**
St. Petersburg Museum
of History **10**

Yellow Shuttle (☎ 727/525-3333) offers 24-hour van service between the airport and any St. Petersburg area destination or hotel. The flat-rate, one-way fare is $12 to any St. Pete or gulf beach destination. **Yellow Cab Taxis** (☎ 727/799-2222) line up outside baggage-claim areas. Average taxi fare from the airport to St. Petersburg or any of the gulf beaches is about $25 to $35.

Amtrak (☎ 800/USA-RAIL for reservations) has rail service to Tampa with bus connections to downtown St. Petersburg (see "Getting There & Getting Around," in chapter 1).

VISITOR INFORMATION

For advance information about both St. Petersburg and the beaches, contact the **St. Petersburg/Clearwater Area Convention & Visitors Bureau,** 14450 46th St. N., Clearwater, FL 34622 (☎ 800/345-6710, or 727/464-7200 for advance hotel reservations; fax 727/464-7222; www.stpete-clearwater.com). The office is south of Roosevelt Boulevard (Fla. 686) opposite St. Petersburg–Clearwater International Airport.

A wealth of information is also available from the **St. Petersburg Area Chamber of Commerce,** 100 2nd Ave. N. (at 1st Street), St. Petersburg, FL 33701 (☎ 727/821-4069; fax 727/895-6326; www.stpete.com). This downtown main office and visitors center is open Monday to Friday from 8am to 5pm, Saturday 9am to 4pm, Sunday noon to 3pm. Ask for a copy of the chamber's visitor guide, which lists hotels, motels, condominiums, and other accommodations.

Also downtown, there are **walk-in information centers** on the first level of The Pier and in the lobby of the Florida International Museum (see "Seeing the Top Attractions," below).

The chamber also operates the **Suncoast Welcome Center** (☎ 727/573-1449), on Ulmerton Road at Exit 18 southbound off I-275 (there's no exit here for northbound traffic). Open daily from 9am to 5pm except New Year's Day, Easter, Thanksgiving, and Christmas.

2 Getting Around

A free trolley service operates between The Pier and the parking lots on shore, where you can connect to the **Looper: the Downtown Trolley** (☎ 727/571-3440), which runs out to the end of The Pier and past all of the downtown attractions every 30 minutes from 11am to 5pm daily except Thanksgiving and Christmas. Rides cost 50¢ per person.

The **Pinellas Suncoast Transit Authority/PSTA** (☎ 727/ 530-9911) operates regular bus service throughout Pinellas County.

If you need a cab, call **Yellow Cab** (☎ 727/821-7777) or **Independent Cab** (☎ 727/327-3444).

Pierside Rentals, on The Pier (☎ 727/822-8697), rents bicycles and in-line skates for $5 an hour, $25 a day.

3 Seeing the Top Attractions

Florida Holocaust Museum. 55 5th St. S. (between Central Ave. and 1st St. S.). ☎ **727/820-0100.** www.flholocaustmuseum.org. Admission $6 adults, $5 seniors. Mon–Fri 10am–5pm, Sat–Sun noon–5pm. Closed Rosh Hashanah, Yom Kippur, and Christmas.

This thought-provoking museum has exhibits about the Holocaust, including a boxcar used to transport human cargo to the Auschwitz death camp in Poland. Its main focus, however, is to promote tolerance and understanding in the present. It was founded by Walter P. Loebenberg, a local businessman who escaped Nazi Germany in 1939 and fought with the U.S. Army in World War II.

Florida International Museum. 100 2nd St. N. (between 1st and 2nd aves. N.). ☎ **877/535-7469** or 727/822-3693. www.floridamuseum.org. Admission $13.95 adults, $12.95 seniors, $5.95 children 6–18, free for children under 6. Daily 9am–7pm.

This facility attracted 600,000 visitors from around the world when it opened its first exhibition in 1995, and the success has continued (its recent exhibits on the *Titanic*, the Incas, and President John F. Kennedy were smash hits). Call to see what's scheduled during your visit. The museum is housed in the former Maas Brothers Department Store, long an area landmark. Tickets should be reserved and purchased in advance to be sure of a specific time. Each visitor is equipped with an audio guide as part of the admission price; allow at least 2 hours to tour a major exhibition. There's an excellent museum store here.

Museum of Fine Arts. 255 Beach Dr. NE (at 3rd Ave. N.). ☎ **727/896-2667.** Admission Mon–Sat $6 adults, $5 seniors, $2 students. Admission free on Sun (donation suggested). Mon–Sat 10am–5pm, Sun 1–5pm; winter, third Thurs of each month 10am–9pm. Closed Mon July–Sept, New Year's Day, Thanksgiving, and Christmas.

Resembling a Mediterranean villa on the waterfront, this museum houses a permanent collection of European, American, pre-Colombian, and Far Eastern art, with works by such artists as

Fragonard, Monet, Renoir, Cézanne, and Gauguin. Other highlights include period rooms with antiques and historical furnishings, plus a gallery of Steuben crystal, a new decorative-arts gallery, and world-class rotating exhibits. Ask about classical music performances from October to April.

The Pier. 800 2nd Ave. NE. ☎ **727/821-6164.** www.stpete-pier.com. Free admission to all the public areas and decks; donations welcome at the Pier Aquarium. Great Explorations $4, $2 seniors, free for children under 3. Valet parking $6, self-parking $3. Pier Mon–Thurs 10am–9pm, Fri–Sat 10am–10pm, Sun 11am–7pm. Aquarium Mon–Sat 10am–8pm, Sun noon–6pm. Great Explorations Mon–Fri 9am–5pm. Shops and restaurant hours vary.

Walk or ride out on The Pier and enjoy this festive waterfront dining and shopping complex overlooking Tampa Bay. Originally built as a railroad pier in 1889, today it's capped by a spaceship-like inverted pyramid offering five levels of shops and restaurants, a tourist information desk, observation deck, catwalks for fishing, boat docks, miniature golf, boat and water-sports rentals, sight-seeing boats, and a food court, plus an aquarium and a hands-on children's museum. You can rent boats and go on cruises from here (see "Outdoor Pursuits & Spectator Sports," below).

If it's still here (plans were in the works to move to a new location), **Great Explorations Hands-On Museum** offers a variety of hands-on exhibits—great for a rainy day or for kids who've overdosed on the sun and need to cool off indoors. They can explore a long, dark tunnel; measure their strength, flexibility, and fitness; paint a work of art with sunlight; and play a melody with a sweep of the hand.

✪ **Salvador Dalí Museum.** 1000 3rd St. S. (near 11th Ave. S.). ☎ **727/823-3767.** www.daliweb.com. Admission $9 adults, $7 seniors, $5 students, free for children 9 and under. 50% discount Thurs 5–8pm. Mon–Wed 9:30am–5:30pm, Thurs 9:30am–8pm, Fri–Sat 9:30am–5:30pm, Sun noon–5:30pm. Closed Thanksgiving and Christmas.

Located on Tampa Bay about 7 blocks south of The Pier (look for Dalí's huge signature slashed across the white building), this starkly modern museum houses the world's largest collection of works by the renowned Spanish surrealist. It includes 94 oil paintings, more than 100 watercolors and drawings, and 1,300 graphics, plus posters, photos, sculptures, objets d'art, and a 5,000-volume library on Dalí and surrealism. An Ohio plastic engineer Reynolds Morse and his wife, Eleanore, discovered the (some say mad) Catalonian artist and began collecting his works in 1943. They moved the collection here in 1980. Docents are on hand to explain the artist's works, including his famous flaccid clocks. Dalí drew himself into many of his paintings and drawings; be on the lookout for his handlebar mustache. There also are special exhibits of works by other famous artists four times a year.

St. Petersburg Museum of History. 335 2nd Ave. NE. ☎ **727/894-1052.** Admission $5 adults, $4 seniors, $2 children 7–17, free for children 6 and under. Mon–Sat 10am–5pm, Sun 1–5pm.

Located at the foot of The Pier, this museum chronicles St. Petersburg's history with artifacts, documents, clothing, photographs, and computer stations where you can "flip through the past." The most interesting exhibit is a replica of the Benoist airboat, which made the world's first scheduled commercial flight from St. Petersburg in 1914.

4 Outdoor Pursuits & Spectator Sports

You can get up-to-the-minute recorded information about the city's sports and recreational activities by calling the **Leisure Line** (☎ 727/893-7500).

BIKING

With miles of flat terrain, the St. Petersburg area is ideal for bikers, in-line skaters, and hikers. The **Pinellas Trail** is especially good, since it follows an abandoned railroad bed 47 miles from St. Petersburg north to Tarpon Springs (and from there to Tampa). The St. Pete trailhead is on 34th Street South (U.S. 19), between 8th and Fairfield Avenues south. It's packed on the weekends. Free strip maps of the trail are available at the St. Petersburg Area Chamber of Commerce (see "Visitor Information," above).

BOAT RENTALS

On The Pier, **Pierside Rentals** (☎ 727/363-0000) rents Wave Runners and jet boats. Prices for Wave Runners begin at $45 for an hour; for jet boats, from $55 per 30 minutes. Open daily from 10am to 9pm.

CRUISING

The *Caribbean Queen* (☎ 727/895-BOAT) departs from The Pier and offers 1-hour sightseeing and dolphin-watching cruises around Tampa Bay. Sailings are daily at 1, 3, and 5pm; they cost $10 for adults, $8 for seniors and juniors 12 to 17, $5 for children 3 to 11, and free for children 2 and under.

GOLF

One of the nation's top 50 municipal courses, the ✪ **Mangrove Bay Golf Course,** 875 62nd Ave. NE (☎ **727/893-7797**), hugs the inlets of Old Tampa Bay and offers an 18-hole, par-72 course. Facilities include a driving range; lessons and golf-club rental are also available. Fees are about $22, $32 including a cart in winter, slightly lower off-season. Open daily from 6:30am to 6pm.

The city also operates the **Twin Brooks Golf Course,** 3800 22nd Ave. S. (☎ **727/893-7445**).

In Largo, the **Bardmoor Golf Club,** 7919 Bardmoor Blvd. (☎ **727/397-0483**), is often the venue for major tournaments. Lakes punctuate 17 of the 18 holes on this par-72 championship course. Lessons and rental clubs are available, as is a Tom Fazio-designed practice range. Call the clubhouse for seasonal greens fees. Open daily from 7am to dusk.

Adjacent to the St. Petersburg–Clearwater airport, the **Airco Flite Golf Course,** 3650 Roosevelt Blvd., Clearwater (☎ **727/573-4653**), is a championship 18-hole, par-72 course with a driving range. Golf-club rentals are also available. Greens fees including cart range from $25 to $35 in winter, about $20 off-season. Open daily from 7am to 6pm.

Call **Tee Times USA** (☎ **800/374-8633**) to reserve times at these and other area courses.

If you want to take up golf or sharpen your game, TV "Golf Doctor" Joe Quinzi hosts his **Quinzi Golf Academy** (☎ **727/725-1999**) at the Safety Harbor Resort and Spa (see "Where to Stay," below). His school offers personalized instructions and clinics.

SAILING

The **Annapolis Sailing School,** 6800 Sunshine Skyway Lane S. (☎ **800/638-9192** or 727/867-8102; www.annapolissailing.com), almost at the foot of the Sunshine Skyway bridge, can teach you to sail or perfect your sailing skills. Various courses are offered at this branch of the famous Maryland-based school, lasting 2, 5, or 8 days. Call for prices and schedules.

The school is based at the **Holiday Inn SunSpree Resort,** 6800 Sunshine Skyway Lane S., St. Petersburg, FL 33711 (☎ **800/227-8045** or 727/867-1151), a recently renovated motel with an expansive bayside pool area.

SPECTATOR SPORTS

St. Petersburg has always been a baseball town, and **Tropicana Field,** a 45,000-seat domed stadium alongside I-175 between 9th and 16th streets south, is the home of the American League **Tampa Bay Devil Rays** (☎ 727/898-RAYS; www.devilrays. com). The baseball season runs from April through September. Call for schedule and ticket information. The Devil Rays move outdoors to Al Lang Stadium, on 2nd Avenue South at 1st Street South (☎ **727/825-3137** or 727/825-3250), for their spring training games from mid-February through March. The Devil Ray's minor league team, the **St. Petersburg Devil Rays** (☎ 727/822-3384; www.stpetedevilrays.com), play in Al Lang Stadium from April through August.

TENNIS

You can learn to play or hone your game at the **Phil Green Tennis Academy** at Safety Harbor Resort and Spa (see "Where to Stay," below).

5 Shopping

The Pier, at the end of 2nd Avenue NE (☎ **727/821-6164**), houses more than a dozen boutiques and craft shops, but nearby Beach Drive, running along the waterfront, is one of the most fashionable downtown strolling and shopping venues.

Central Avenue is another shopping area, featuring the **Gas Plant Antique Arcade,** between 12th and 13th streets (☎ **727/ 895-0368**), the largest antique mall on Florida's west coast, with over 100 dealers displaying their wares. The **Florida Craftsmen Gallery,** at 5th Street (☎ 727/821-7391), is a showcase for the works of more than 150 Florida artisans and craftspeople: jewelry, ceramics, woodwork, fiber works, glassware, paper creations, and metalwork.

In the suburbs, outlet shoppers can browse BonWorth, Dress Barn, Van Heusen, Bugle Boy, L'eggs, Bass Shoes, T.J. Maxx, and more at the air-conditioned **Bay Area Outlet Mall,** at the inter-section of U.S. 19 and East Bay Drive (☎ **727/535-2337**).

6 Where to Stay

Ask the **St. Petersburg Area Chamber of Commerce** (see "Essentials," above) for a copy of its visitor guide, which lists a wide range of hotels, motels, condominiums, and other accommodations.

The **St. Petersburg/Clearwater Area Convention & Visitors Bureau** (see "Visitor Information," above) publishes a brochure, listing members of its Superior Small Lodging program; all with less than 50 rooms, they have been inspected and certified for cleanliness and value. In addition, the bureau has a free **reservations service** (☎ 800/345-6710).

You'll find plenty of chain motels along U.S. 19.

With regard to prices, the high season is from January to April. The hotel tax rate in Pinellas County is 11%.

VERY EXPENSIVE

✪ **Renaissance Vinoy Resort.** 501 5th Ave. NE (at Beach Dr.), St. Petersburg, FL 33701. ☎ **800/HOTELS-1** or 727/894-1000. Fax 727/822-2785. 360 units. A/C MINIBAR TV TEL. Winter $289–$349 double. Off-season $139–$289 double. AE, DC, DISC, MC, V. Valet parking $12; self-parking $8.

Built as the grand Vinoy Park in 1925, this elegant Spanish-style establishment reopened in 1992 after a total and meticulous $93 million restoration that has made it more luxurious than ever. Dominating the northern part of downtown, it overlooks Tampa Bay and is within walking distance of The Pier, Central Avenue, museums, and other attractions. All the guest rooms, many of which enjoy lovely views of the bay front, are designed to offer the utmost in comfort and include three phones, an additional TV in the bathroom, bath scales, and more. Units in the new Tower wing have balconies and some have whirlpools.

Dining/Diversions: Marchand's Grille, an elegant, Mediterranean-style room overlooking the bay, serves the best steaks, seafood, and chops in town. The Terrace Room is the main dining room for breakfast, lunch, and dinner. Casual lunches and dinners are available at the indoor-outdoor Alfresco, near the pool deck, and at the Clubhouse at the golf course on Snell Isle. There are also two bar/lounges.

Amenities: Concierge, 24-hour room service, laundry service, tour desk, child care, complimentary coffee and newspaper with wake-up call. Two swimming pools (connected by a roaring waterfall), 14-court tennis complex (11 lighted), 18-hole private championship golf course on nearby Snell Isle, private 74-slip marina, two croquet courts, fitness center (with sauna, steam room, spa, massage, and exercise equipment), access to two bay-side beaches, shuttle service to gulf beaches, hair salon, gift shop.

MODERATE

Bay Gables Bed & Breakfast. 136 4th Ave. NE (between Beach Dr. and 1st St. N), St. Petersburg, FL 33701. ☎ **800/822-8803** or 727/822-8855. Fax 727/824-7223. 9 units. A/C TV TEL. Winter $85–$135 double. Off-season $65–$105 double. Rates include continental breakfast. AE, MC, V.

You can walk to The Pier from this charming B&B with wrap-around porches on all three of its stories. Built in the 1930s, it overlooks a flower-filled garden with a gazebo. The guest quarters have been furnished with ceiling fans and Victorian pieces, including a canopy bed in one room. The honeymoon suite is equipped with a large double shower, Jacuzzi, and bidet; the rest have both claw-foot tubs and modern showers in their bathrooms. Half of the rooms open to the porches, while the rest have a separate sitting room and kitchenette. Continental breakfast is served in a restaurant next door. This is a professionally managed operation; the owners don't live on the premises.

✪ The Heritage Holiday Inn. 234 3rd Ave. N. (between 2nd and 3rd sts.), St. Petersburg, FL 33701. ☎ **800/283-7829** or 727/822-4814. Fax 727/823-1644. www.holidayinnstpete.com. 71 units. A/C TV TEL. $97–$139 double. AE, DC, DISC, MC, V.

No ordinary Holiday Inn, The Heritage dates from the early 1920s and is the closest thing to a Southern mansion you'll find in the heart of downtown. With a sweeping veranda, French doors, and tropical courtyard, it attracts an eclectic clientele, from young families to seniors. The furnishings include period antiques. There's a heated swimming pool and a whirlpool in a small tropical courtyard between the main building and a restaurant next door. Amenities include limited room service and valet laundry.

Mansion House Bed & Breakfast. 105 5th Ave. NE (at 1st St. N.), St. Petersburg, FL 33701. ☎ **800/274-7520** or 727/821-9391. Fax 727/821-9391 (same as phone). www.mansionbandb.com. 10 units (all with bathroom). A/C TV TEL. Winter $110–$165 double. Off-season $95–$165 double. Rates include full breakfast. AE, MC, V.

Mirror images of each other, these two Craftsman-style houses, separated by a landscaped courtyard, were built in 1904 and 1912 by a local doctor (one house served as his office). The comfortable living room in the main house, which has 6 of the 10 units here, opens to a sunroom, off which a small screened porch provides mosquito-free lounging and the only place where guests can smoke. Both houses have upstairs front parlors with TVs, VCRs, and libraries. Tall, old-fashioned windows let lots of light into the attractive guest rooms, in which some furniture has been decorated by a local artist. The "Pembrooke" room actually is upstairs over the carriage house; it has its own refrigerator, phone, TV, and four-poster bed with mosquito net. In an unusual architectural twist, the "Harlech" room has a toilet and hand basin in one converted closet, a shower in another. Proprietors Rob and Rosie Ray serve a full breakfast in two formal dining rooms and keep fruit bowls and snacks available at all hours in both houses. There's a whirlpool bath in its own screened hut in the backyard.

St. Petersburg Hilton. 333 1st St. S. (between 3rd and 4th aves. S.), St. Petersburg, FL 33701. ☎ **800/HILTONS** or 727/894-5000. Fax 727/823-4797. 333 units. A/C TV TEL. Winter $169–$195 double. Off-season $129–$139 double. Packages available. Valet parking $8; no self parking. AE, DC, MC, V.

This 15-story business and convention hotel is within steps of the Salvador Dalí Museum, Al Lang Field, and the Bayfront Center's theaters. Otherwise, views from the upper-floor rooms are its main draw for casual travelers. The bedrooms are furnished with traditional dark woods and floral fabrics. A full-service restaurant specializes in continental cuisine, while a deli provides light fare and Pizza Hut pies. A lobby bar has piano entertainment. Facilities include an outdoor heated swimming pool, whirlpool, health club with a sauna, and gift shop.

A NEARBY SPA

✪ **Safety Harbor Resort and Spa.** 105 N. Bayshore Dr., Safety Harbor, FL 34695. ☎ **888/BEST-SPA** or 727/726-1161. Fax 727/724-7749. www.safetyharborspa.com. E-mail: safety.harbor@ssrc.com. 193 units. Winter $129–$199 double. Off-season $89–$129 double. Packages available. AE, DC, DISC, MC, V. Valet parking $4, free self-parking. Pets accepted at extra charge.

Hernando de Soto thought he had found Ponce de Léon's fabled Fountain of Youth when he happened upon five mineral springs here on the shores of Old Tampa Bay in 1539. You won't get your youth back at this venerable spa, which has been in operation since 1926 and got a face-lift in 1998, but you are in for some serious pampering, from massages to hydrotherapy, and a full menu of fitness classes from boxing to yoga. The springs enable the spa to offer acclaimed water-fitness programs. This is also a good place to work on your games at the Quinzi Golf Academy and the Phil Green Tennis Academy (see "Outdoor Activities & Spectator Sports," above). The sprawling complex of beige stucco buildings with Spanish tile roofs sits on 22 waterfront acres in the sleepy town of Safety Harbor, north of St. Petersburg. Moss-draped

Safety Harbor has a charming, small-town ambience, with a number of shops and restaurants just outside the spa's entrance.

Dining: Nutritious menus emphasizing American fusion cuisine use lots of Florida ingredients in both the Spa Dining Room and the resort's cafe, which is open to the public for lunch and dinner.

Amenities: Concierge, limited room service, valet laundry, guest laundry, valet parking, Clarins Skin Institute, 50,000-square-foot spa and fitness center, three heated pools, nine lighted tennis courts, bike rentals, business center, beauty salon, boutiques.

7 Where to Dine

Don't overlook the food court at **The Pier,** where the inexpensive chow is accompanied by a very rich, but quite free, view of the bay. Among The Pier's restaurants is a branch of Tampa's famous **Columbia** (☎ 727/822-8000). Downtown also has an off-shoot of Ybor City's **Ovo Cafe,** at 515 Central Ave. (☎ 727/895-5515). See "Where to Dine" in chapter 2 for details about Columbia and Ovo Cafe.

MODERATE

Garden Bistro. 217 Central Ave. (between 2nd and 3rd Sts.). ☎ **727/896-3800.** Reservations recommended for dinner. Burgers $6; main courses $9–$17. AE, DISC, MC, V. Daily noon–2am. MEDITERRANEAN/AMERICAN.

This lively restaurant combines European ambience with Mediterranean-influenced cuisine. Choice seats are under huge shade trees in the garden, screened from the street by a trellis fence. Inside, the decor blends the American Southwest with the Mediterranean, with arches, a 19th-century tiled floor, modern local art, and lots of flowers and plants. The menu stars pastas such as shrimp and prosciutto, spinach, tomatoes, olive oil, and garlic over linguine. Hamburgers are available at lunch and dinner. On Friday and Saturday, live jazz adds to the ambience from 9pm to 1am.

Keystone Club. 320 4th St. N. (between 3rd and 4th aves. N.). ☎ **727/822-6600.** Reservations recommended. Main courses $12–$24; early bird specials $10. AE, DC, DISC, MC, V. Mon–Fri 11am–2:30pm and 5–10pm, Sat 4–10pm, Sun 4–9pm. Early bird specials winter only, Mon–Fri 4:30–5:30pm, Sat–Sun 4–5:30pm. STEAKS/PRIME RIB.

Resembling an exclusive men's club, this cozy restaurant's forest-green walls accented by dark wood and etched glass create an atmosphere that's reminiscent of a Manhattan-style chophouse. But women are also welcome to partake of the beef, which is king here. Specialties include roast prime rib, New York strip steak, and filet mignon. Seafood also makes an appearance, with fresh lobster and grouper at market price. During winter, "sunset" early bird specials include lunch-size portions, a beverage, and dessert.

INEXPENSIVE

✪ **Fourth Street Shrimp Store.** 1006 4th St. N. (at 10th Ave. N.). ☎ **727/ 822-0325.** Reservations not accepted. Sandwiches $2.50–$7; main courses $4.50–$13. MC, V. Sun–Thurs 11am–9pm, Fri–Sat 11am–10pm. SEAFOOD.

If you're anywhere in the area, don't miss at least driving by to see the colorful, cartoonlike mural on the outside of this eclectic establishment just north of downtown. On first impression it looks like graffiti, but it's actually a gigantic drawing of people eating. Inside, it gets even better, with paraphernalia and murals on two walls making the main dining room seem like a warehouse with windows looking out on an early-19th-century seaport (one painted sailor permanently peers in to see what you're eating). You'll pass a seafood market counter when you enter, from which comes the fresh namesake shrimp, the star here. You can also pick from grouper, clam strips, catfish, or oysters fried, broiled, or steamed, all served in heaping portions. This is the best and certainly the most interesting bargain in town.

The Moon Under Water. 332 Beach Dr. (between 3rd and 4th aves.). ☎ **727/ 896-6160.** Reservations accepted only for groups. Sandwiches and salads $6–$8; main courses $8–$16. AE, DC, DISC, MC, V. Daily 11:30am–11pm. Closed New Year's Day, Thanksgiving, Christmas. ASIAN/MIDDLE EASTERN.

The British raj rules supreme at this pub facing the bayfront park. You can choose a table on the veranda out front, or inside the darkly paneled dining room with a host of slowly twirling fans hung from the ceiling and a plethora of colonial artifacts along the walls, including obligatory pith helmets. Your taste buds are in for a treat here, for the menu covers a number of former British outposts, including America (burgers and Philly cheese steaks), but the emphasis here is on mild, medium, or blazing hot Indian curries—with a recommended wine or cold Irish, British, or Australian beer to cool the taste buds. For lighter fare, consider mid-eastern tabbouleh. There's entertainment Friday and Saturday evenings.

8   St. Petersburg After Dark

Good sources of nightlife information are the Friday "Weekend" section of the *St. Petersburg Times*, the "Baylife" and "Friday Extra" sections of the *Tampa Tribune*, and the *Weekly Planet*, a tabloid available at the visitor information offices and in many hotel and restaurant lobbies. The bimonthly magazine *Event Guide Tampa Bay* gives a rundown on what's going on.

THE CLUB & MUSIC SCENE

A historic attraction as well as an entertainment venue, the Moorish-style **Coliseum Ballroom,** 535 4th Ave. N. (☎ 727/892-5202), has been hosting dancing, big bands, boxing, and other events since 1924 (it even made an appearance in the 1985 movie *Cocoon*). Come out and watch the town's many seniors doing the jitterbug just like it was 1945 again! Call for the schedule and prices.

PERFORMING ARTS VENUES

Tropicana Field, 1 Stadium Dr. (☎ 727/825-3100), has a capacity of 50,000 for major concerts, but also hosts a variety of smaller events when the Devil Rays aren't playing baseball.

The Bayfront Center, 400 1st St. S. (☎ **727/892-5767,** or 727/892-5700 for recorded information), houses the 8,100-seat Bayfront Arena and the 2,000-seat Mahaffey Theater. The schedule includes a variety of concerts, Broadway shows, big bands, ice shows, and circus performances.

4

The St. Pete & Clearwater Beaches

*I*f you're looking for sun and sand, you'll find plenty of both on the 28 miles of slim barrier islands that skirt the gulf shore of the Pinellas Peninsula. With some one million visitors coming here every year, don't be surprised if you have lots of company. But you'll also discover quieter neighborhoods geared to families, and this area has some of the nation's finest beaches, which are protected from development by parks and nature preserves.

At the southern end of the strip, St. Pete Beach is the granddaddy of the area's resorts. In fact, visitors started coming here nearly a century ago, and they haven't quit. Today St. Pete Beach is heavily developed and often overcrowded during the winter season. If you like high-rises and mile-a-minute action, St. Pete Beach is for you. But even here, Pass-a-Grille, on the island's southern end, is a quiet residential enclave with eclectic shops and a fine public beach.

A gentler lifestyle begins just to the north on 3¹/₂-mile-long Treasure Island. From there, you cross famous John's Pass to Sand Key, a 12-mile island occupied by primarily residential Madeira Beach, Redington Beach, North Redington Beach, Redington Shores, Indian Shores, Indian Rocks Beach, and Belleair Beach. Finally the road crosses a soaring bridge to Clearwater Beach, whose silky sands attract active families and couples.

If you like your great outdoors unfettered by development, the jewels here are Fort Desoto Park, down below St. Pete Beach at the mouth of Tampa Bay, and Caladesi Island State Park, north of Clearwater Beach. They are consistently rated among America's top beaches. And Sand Key Park, looking at Clearwater Beach from the southern shores of Little Pass, is one of Florida's finest local beach parks.

1   Orientation

ARRIVING

To reach St. Pete Beach and Treasure Island from I-275, take Exit 4 and follow the Pinellas Bayway (Fla. 682) west (50¢ toll). For Indian Rocks Beach, take Exit 18 and follow Ulmerton Road due west to the gulf. For the Redington beaches, take Exit 15 and follow Gandy and Park boulevards (Fla. 694) due west (Park Boulevard also is known as 74th Avenue North). For Clearwater Beach, take the Courtney Campbell Causeway (Fla. 60) west from Tampa; the Causeway becomes Gulf-to-Bay Boulevard (also Fla. 60), which leads straight west into Clearwater.

See "Getting There" in chapters 1 and 2 for information about flights to, and transportation from, Tampa International and St. Petersburg–Clearwater International airports.

VISITOR INFORMATION

See "Visitor Information" in section 1 of chapter 3 for the St. Petersburg/Clearwater Area Convention & Visitors Bureau and the St. Petersburg Area Chamber of Commerce. You can get information specific to the beaches from the **Gulf Beaches of Tampa Bay Chamber of Commerce,** 6990 Gulf Blvd. (at 70th Avenue), St. Pete Beach, FL 33706 (☎ **800/944-1847** or 727/360-6957; fax 727/360-2233; www.gulfbeaches-tampabay. com; e-mail: gulfbchs@gte.net). The chamber's visitors center is open Monday to Friday from 9am to 5pm.

For advance information about Clearwater Beach, contact the **Greater Clearwater Chamber of Commerce,** 128 N. Osceola Ave. (P.O. Box 2457), Clearwater, FL 34615 (☎ **727/461-0011**). You can also walk into the **Clearwater Tourist Information Center,** on Causeway Boulevard in the Clearwater Beach Marina Building lobby (☎ **727/462-6531**). It's open daily in winter from 9am to 5pm, off-season Monday to Saturday from 9am to 5pm, Sunday from 1 to 5pm.

2   Getting Around

BATS City Transit (☎ 727/367-3086) offers bus service along the St. Pete Beach strip. BATS connects with the **Treasure Island Transit System** (☎ 727/547-4575), which runs buses along the Treasure Island, at Egan Park. The fare on either system is $1.

ACCOMMODATIONS ■
Beach Haven **16**
Belleview Biltmore
  Resort & Spa **1**
Best Western Sea
  Stone Resort **27**
Captain's Quarters Inn **8**
Clearwater Beach Hotel **21**
Days Inn Island
  Beach Resort **11**
Don CeSar Beach
  Resort and Spa **17**
Great Heron Inn **4**
Island's End Resort **19**
Palm Pavilion Inn **20**
Pelican—East & West **2**
Radisson Suite Resort
  on Sand Key **29**
Sheraton Sand Key
  Resort **28**
Sirata Beach Resort **14**
Sun West Beach Motel **26**
TradeWinds Resort **13**
Travelodge St. Pete
  Beach **10**

DINING ◆
Beachside Grill **6**
Bob Heilman's
  Beachcomber **23**
Bobby's Bistro
  & Wine Bar **24**
Crabby Bill's **15**
Frenchy's Cafe **22**
Guppy's **3**
Hurricane **18**
Internet Outpost **9**
Lobster Pot **6**
Seafood & Sunsets
  at Julie's **25**
The Salt Rock Grill **5**
Skidder's **12**
The Wine Cellar **7**

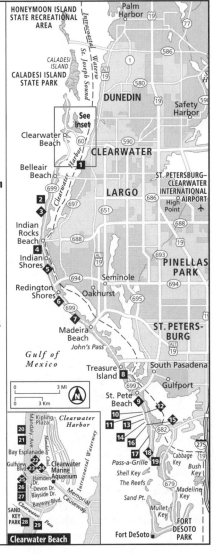

The Gulf Beaches of Tampa Bay Chamber of Commerce has schedules (see "Visitor Information," above).

The **Jolley Trolley** (☎ 727/445-1200) provides service in the Clearwater Beach area, from downtown to the beaches as far south as Sand Key. The ride costs 50¢ per person, 25¢ for seniors.

Along the beach, the major cab company is **BATS Taxi** (☎ 727/367-3702).

3 Hitting the Beach

This entire stretch of coast is one long beach, but since hotels, condominiums, and private homes occupy much of it, you may want to sun and swim at one of the area's public parks. The very best are described below, but there's also the fine **Pass-a-Grille Public Beach,** on the southern end of St. Pete Beach, where you can watch the boats going in and out of Pass-a-Grille Channel and slake your thirst at Hurricane restaurant (see "Where to Dine," below). This and all other Pinellas County public beaches have metered parking lots, so bring a supply of quarters.

The fine ✪ **Sand Key Park,** on the northern tip of Sand Key facing Clearwater Beach, sports a wide beach and gentle surf and is relatively off the beaten path in this commercial area. It's great to get out of the hotel for a morning walk or jog here. Open 8am to dark. Admission is free, but the parking lot has meters. For more information, call ☎ 727/464-3347.

Clearwater Public Beach (also known as Pier 60) has beach volleyball, water-sports rentals, lifeguards, rest rooms, showers, and concessions. The swimming is excellent, and there's a children's playground and a fishing pier with bait and tackle shop. Gated municipal parking lots here cost $1 per hour or $7 a day. The lots are right across the street from Clearwater Beach Marina, a prime base for boating, cruises, and other waterborne activities (see "Outdoor Activities," below).

CALADESI ISLAND STATE PARK

Occupying a 3¹/₂-mile island north of Clearwater Beach, ✪ **Caladesi Island State Park** boasts one of Florida's top beaches, a lovely, relatively secluded stretch with fine soft sand edged in sea grass and palmettos. Dolphins cavort in the waters offshore. In the park itself, there's a nature trail, and you might see one of the rattlesnakes, black racers, raccoons, armadillos, or rabbits that live here. A concession stand, ranger station, and bathhouses (with rest rooms and showers) are available. Caladesi Island is accessible only by ferry from **Honeymoon Island State Recreation Area,** which is connected by Causeway Boulevard (Fla. 586) to Dunedin, north of Clearwater. You'll first have to pay the admission to Honeymoon Island: $4 per vehicle with two to eight occupants, $2 per single-occupant vehicle, $1 for pedestrians and bicyclists. Beginning daily at 10am, the ferry departs Honeymoon Island every hour on winter weekdays, every 30 minutes on summer weekdays, and every 30 minutes on weekends year-round. Roundtrip rides cost $6 for adults and $3.50 for kids.

The two parks are open daily from 8am to sunset and are administered by Gulf Islands Geopark, No. 1 Causeway Blvd., Dunedin, FL 34698 (☎ **727/469-5942;** http://www.dep.state. fl.us/parks/District_4/Caladesi/ and http://www.dep.state.fl.us/parks/District_4/HoneymoonIsland/).

FORT DESOTO PARK

South of St. Pete Beach at the very mouth of Tampa Bay, ✪ **Fort Desoto Park** encompasses a group of five connected barrier islands set aside by Pinellas County as a 900-acre bird, animal, and plant sanctuary. Besides the stunning white-sugar sand beach (where you can watch the manatees and dolphins play offshore), there's a Spanish American War–era fort, great fishing from piers, large playgrounds for kids, and 4 miles of trails winding through the park for in-line skaters, bicyclists, and joggers.

Sitting by itself on a heavily forested island, the park's 233 campsites usually are sold out, especially on weekends. To make reservations, you must appear in person and pay for your site no more than 30 days in advance at the campground office, at 631 Chestnut St. in Clearwater, or at 150 5th St. North in downtown St. Petersburg. You must reserve for at least 2 nights, but you can stay no more than 14 nights in any 30-day period. Sites cost $23.21 a night, including tax. All have water and electricity hookups.

Admission to the park is free. It's open daily from 8am to dusk, although campers and persons fishing from the piers can stay later. To get here, take the Pinellas Byway (50¢ toll) east from St. Pete Beach and follow Fla. 679 (35¢ toll) and the signs south to the park. For more information, contact the park at 3500 Pinellas Bayway, Tierra Verde, FL 33715 (☎ **727/582-2267**).

4   Outdoor Activities

BICYCLING & IN-LINE SKATING

With miles of flat terrain and paved roads, the beach area is ideal for bikers and in-line skaters, and the 47-mile-long Pinellas Trail runs close by on the mainland (see "Outdoor Activities & Spectator Sports," in chapter 2). In St. Pete Beach, you can rent bicycles, skates, and scooters from **Beach Cyclist Sports Center,** 7517 Blind Pass Rd. (☎ **727/367-5001**). **East End Bike Rentals** (☎ **727/398-4811**) has them at John's Pass Village in Madeira Beach. In Clearwater Beach, contact **Transportation Station,** 652 Gulfview Blvd. (☎ **727/443-3188**). Bikes at all three range from about $5 per hour to $20 a day; scooters, about $13 an hour to $40 per day.

BOATING, FISHING & OTHER WATER SPORTS

You can indulge in parasailing, boating, deep-sea fishing, wave running, sightseeing, dolphin watching, waterskiing, and just about any other waterborne diversion your heart could desire here. All you have to do is head to one of two beach locations: **Hubbard's Marina,** at John's Pass Village and Boardwalk (☎ **727/393-1947**), in Madeira Beach on the southern tip of Sand Key; or **Clearwater Beach Marina,** at Coronado Drive and Causeway Boulevard (☎ **800/772-4479** or 727/461-3133), which is at the beach end of the causeway leading to downtown Clearwater. Agents in booths there will give you the schedules and prices (they are approximately the same at both locations), answer any questions you have, and make reservations if necessary. Go in the early morning to set up today's activities, or in the afternoon to book tomorrow's.

CRUISES

The top nature cruise here is a ✪ **Sea Life Safari** (☎ **800/ 444-4814** or 727/462-2628) operated by the Clearwater Marine Aquarium (see "Attractions on Land," below). These $2^1/_2$-hour "sealife safaris" are more like field trips than pleasure cruises. Aquarium biologists go along to explain what they pull up in trawl nets (don't worry: they throw it all back). You'll see birds and other wildlife on a visit to a bird sanctuary islet. Dolphin sightings are likely, too. The cruises leave from the aquarium daily at 12:30 and 3:15pm, from Clearwater Beach Marina at 10am, 12:45, and 3:15pm. They cost $13.95 for adults, $9 for kids 3 to

12. You can combine the cruise with aquarium admission and save $3. Call to confirm the schedule and reserve. Also ask about sunset nature cruises from mid-April to mid-October.

For a quick ride to Shell Key take the **Shell Key Shuttle,** Merry Pier, on Pass-a-Grille Way at the eastern end of 8th Avenue in southern St. Pete Beach (☎ **727/360-1348**). Boats leave daily at 10am, noon, and 2pm. Prices are $12 for adults, $6 for children 12 and under. The ride takes 15 minutes, and you can return on any shuttle you wish.

The most unusual outings here are with **Captain Memo's Pirate Cruise,** at Clearwater Beach Marina (☎ **727/446-2587;** www.pirateflorida.com), which sails the *Pirate's Ransom,* a repro-duction of a pirate ship, on 2-hour daytime "pirate cruises" as well as sunset and evening champagne cruises. Cruises operate year-round, daily at 10am and 2, 4:30, and 7pm. For adults, daytime or sunset cruises cost $27; evening cruises, $30; both daytime and evening cruises cost $20 for seniors and juniors 13 to 17, $17 for children 2 to 12, free for children under 2.

Two paddle-wheel riverboats operate here: The *Show Queen* has lunch, sunset dinner, and Sunday brunch cruises from Clear-water Beach Marina (☎ **727/461-3113;** www.marinetours.com). The *Starlite Princess* does likewise from 3400 Pasadena Ave. S. (☎ **727/462-2628;** www.starlitecruises.com), at the eastern side of the Corey Causeway linking St. Pete Beach to the mainland. Call for schedules and prices.

5 Attractions on Land

Clearwater Marine Aquarium. 249 Windward Passage, Clearwater. ☎ **888/239-9414** or 727/447-0980. Admission $6.75 adults, $4.25 children 3–11, free for children 2 and under. Mon–Fri 9am–5pm, Sat 9am–4pm, Sun 11am–4pm. The aquarium is off the causeway between Clearwater and Clear-water Beach; follow the signs.

This little jewel of an aquarium on Clearwater Harbor is very low key and friendly; it's dedicated to the rescue and rehabilitation of marine mammals and sea turtles. Exhibits include dolphins, otters, sea turtles, sharks, stingrays, mangroves, and sea grass.

✪ **John's Pass Village and Boardwalk.** 12901 Gulf Blvd. (at John's Pass), Madeira Beach. ☎ **800/944-1847** or 727/397-1511. Free admission. Shops and activities daily 9am–6pm or later.

Casual and charming, this Old Florida fishing village on John's Pass consists of a string of simple wooden structures topped by tin roofs and connected by a 1,000-foot boardwalk. Most of the buildings have been converted into shops, art galleries, restaurants, and saloons. The focal point is the boardwalk and marina, where many water sports are available for visitors (see "Outdoor Activities," above). If you don't go out on the water, this is a great place to have an al fresco lunch—**Sculley's** (☎ 727/393-7749) is the best restaurant here—and watch the boats go in and out of the pass.

✪ **Suncoast Seabird Sanctuary.** 18328 Gulf Blvd., Indian Shores. ☎ **727/391-6211.** Free admission, donations welcome. Daily 9am–dusk. Free tours Wed and Sun 2pm.

At any one time there are usually more than 500 sea and land birds living at the sanctuary, from cormorants, white herons, and birds of prey to the ubiquitous brown pelican. The nation's largest wild-bird hospital, dedicated to the rescue, repair, recuperation, and release of sick and injured wild birds, is also here.

6 Shopping

John's Pass Village and Boardwalk, on John's Pass in Madeira Beach (see "Attractions on Land," above), has an unremarkable collection of beach souvenir shops, but the atmosphere makes it worth a stroll. The pick of the lot is the **Bronze Lady** (☎ 727/398-5994), featuring the world's largest collection of works by the late comedian-artist Red Skelton, best known for his numerous clown paintings. The shops are open daily from 9am to 6pm or later.

If you're in the market for some one-of-a-kind hand-hammered jewelry, try **Evander Preston Contemporary Jewelry,** 106 8th Ave., Pass-a-Grille (☎ 727/367-7894), a unique gallery/workshop housed in a 75-year-old building in Pass-a-Grille's block-long 8th Avenue business district. Check out the golden miniature train with diamond headlight (it's not for sale). Open Monday to Saturday from 10am to 5:30pm.

Among the shops in St. Pete Beach's Corey Landings Area, the town's original business strip along 75th Street east of Gulf Boulevard, **The Shell Store** (☎ 727/360-0586) specializes in corals and shells, with an on-premises mini-museum illustrating how they live and grow. There's a good selection of shell home decorations, shell hobbyist supplies, shell art, planters, and jewelry. Open Monday to Saturday from 9:30am to 5pm.

7 Where to Stay

St. Pete Beach and Clearwater Beach have national chain hotels and motels of every name and description. You can also use the St. Petersburg/Clearwater Convention & Visitors Bureau's free **reservations service** (☎ 800/345-6710).

As is the case throughout Florida, there are at least as many rental condominiums here as there are hotel rooms. Many of them are in high-rise buildings right on the beach. Among several local rental agents, **Excell Vacation Condos,** 14955 Gulf Blvd., Madeira Beach, FL 33708 (☎ 800/733-4004 or 727/391-5512; fax 727/393-8885; www.islandtime.com/vacation), and **JC Resort Management,** 17200 Gulf Blvd., North Redington Beach, FL 33708 (☎ 800/535-7776 or 727/397-0441; fax 727/397-8894; www.jcresort.com), have many from which to choose. **Resort Rentals,** 9524 Blind Pass Rd., St. Pete Beach, FL 33707 (☎ 800/293-3979 or 727/363-3336; fax 727/360-5086; www.resort-realty.net), specializes in luxury rental homes.

With regard to prices, high season runs from January to April. Ask about special discounted packages in the summer. Any time of year, though, it's wise to make reservations early. The hotel tax in Pinellas County is 11%.

I have organized accommodations geographically, starting with the congested St. Pete Beach area on the south end of the strip, then the mostly residential Indian Rocks Beach area, then the relatively quiet but still busy Clearwater Beach at the north.

ST. PETE BEACH AREA
VERY EXPENSIVE

✪ **Don CeSar Beach Resort and Spa.** 3400 Gulf Blvd. (at 34th Ave./ Pinellas Byway), St. Pete Beach, FL 33706. ☎ 800/282-1116, 800/ 637-7200, or 727/360-1881. Fax 727/367-6952. www.don-cesar.com. 345 units. A/C MINIBAR TV TEL. Winter $229–$389 double; $304–$699 suite. Off-season $169–$329 double; $239–$699 suite. $7.50 per person per day activities fee. Packages available. AE, DC, DISC, MC, V. Valet parking $10.

Dating froh 1928 and listed on the National Register of Historic Places, this Moorish-style "Pink Palace" tropical getaway is so romantic you may bump into six or seven honeymooning couples in one weekend. Sitting majestically on $7^1/_2$ acres of beachfront, the landmark sports a lobby of classic high windows and archways, crystal chandeliers, marble floors, and original artworks. Most rooms have high ceilings and offer views of the gulf or Boca

Ciega Bay. Some of the 275 rooms under the minarets of the original building may seem rather small by today's standards. If you want more room but less charm, the resort has 70 spacious luxury condos in The Don CeSar Beach House, a mid-rise building $^3/_4$-mile to the north (there's 24-hour complimentary transportation between the two).

Dining/Diversions: The pricey but intimate Maritana Grille can't be beat for fresh gourmet seafood and caviar, if your budget can afford a serious splurge. Other outlets include the King Charles Restaurant (offering a sumptuous Sunday brunch), the Sea Porch Cafe for indoor or outdoor dining by the pool and beach, the Lobby Bar, two beachside bars, and an ice-cream parlor.

Amenities: Concierge, 24-hour room service, valet parking, laundry, newspaper delivery, nightly turndown on request, in-room massage, business services, complimentary coffee in lobby, child care available, children's program, beach, two outdoor heated swimming pools, whirlpool, exercise room, sauna, steam room, volleyball, gift shops, rentals for water-sports equipment, hairdresser, shopping arcade with upscale jewelers and men's and women's resort wear.

EXPENSIVE

Days Inn Island Beach Resort. 6200 Gulf Blvd. (at 62nd Ave.), St. Pete Beach, FL 33706. ☎ **800/544-4222** or 727/367-1902. Fax 727/367-4422. E-mail: daysinnspb@hotmail.com. 102 units. A/C TV TEL. Winter $168–$228 double. Off-season $108–$168 double. AE, DC, DISC, MC, V.

Two long, gray buildings flank a courtyard with heated swimming pool at this beachside property popular with young families. Furnished in dark woods and rich tones, most of the guest rooms have picture-window views of the courtyard. All units have refrigerators and coffeemakers, and about half have kitchenettes. Inside the building, Players Bar & Grille has sports TVs, pizzas, pub fare, and free hot snacks from noon to 7pm daily. Outside, Jimmy B.'s beach bar is a fine place for a sunset cocktail (happy hour runs from noon to 7:30pm) and evening entertainment, including beachside bonfires on Saturdays in winter. Facilities include two outdoor heated swimming pools, volleyball, horseshoes, shuffleboard, and a game room.

Sirata Beach Resort. 5300 Gulf Blvd. (53rd Ave.), St. Pete Beach, FL 33706. ☎ **800/237-0707** or 727/367-2771. Fax 727/360-6799. www.sirata.com.

380 units, including 170 suites. A/C TV TEL. Winter $147–$297 double, $198–$307 suite. Off-season $139–$218 double, $159–$307 suite. AE, DC, DISC, MC, V.

A ton of money was spent in 1999 to completely renovate this older property and bring it up to second-tier status here, almost on a par with its sister hotel, the Tradewinds Resort, but well below the Don Cesar Beach Resort and Spa. In fact, if you've been here before you may not recognize the Sirata from Gulf Boulevard, for a yellow-and-green Old Florida–style facade now disguises the eight-story main building, which houses hotel rooms upstairs (upper-level units have nice views) and a convention center. Meetings and receptions spill out onto a landscaped courtyard nearly enclosed by a U-shaped block of motel rooms. Some guest rooms in this two-story building face the courtyard, but the choice quarters here are its gulf side rooms, the only units here with patios or balconies opening directly to the beach. The most spacious units are efficiencies and one-bedroom suites in two long, two-story buildings set perpendicular to the beach; they all have kitchenettes, but they look out primarily on parking lots.

Dining/Diversions: Dining is not the Sirata's forte (there are plenty of other options within a short walk). On premises are Durango Steakhouse, a daytime deli, and a nighttime sports bar offering snacks and pub grub. You can also order lunches and snacks at bars beside the resort's two attractive swimming pool complexes.

Amenities: Concierge, limited room service, exercise room, games room, business center, children's program, coin laundry, two outdoor swimming pools with whirlpools, volleyball, water sports activities.

TradeWinds Resort. 5500 Gulf Blvd. (at 55th Ave.), St. Pete Beach, FL 33706. ☎ **800/237-0707** or 727/562-1212. Fax 727/562-1222. www. tradewindsresort.com. 577 units. A/C TV TEL. Winter $209–$399 double. Off-season $179–$319 double. Packages available summer and fall. AE, DC, DISC, MC, V. Valet parking $3–$6; free self-parking.

Don't be dismayed by the outward appearance of this six- and seven-story, concrete-and-steel monstrosity, for underneath and beside it runs a maze of brick walkways, patios, and lily ponds connected by a quarter mile of streams. The guest units, which look out on the gulf or the 18 acres of grounds, have up-to-date kitchens or kitchenettes, contemporary furnishings, and private balconies. The children's program and summer packages are a big hit with families from around the world, attracting lots of Europeans.

Dining/Diversions: The top spot for lunch or dinner is the Palm Court, with an Italian-bistro atmosphere; for dinner, there's also Bermudas, a casual family spot. Other food outlets include the Fountain Square Deli, Pizza Hut, and Tropic Treats. Bars include Reflections piano lounge; B.R. Cuda's, with live entertainment and dancing; and the Flying Bridge, a Florida cracker-house-style beachside bar floating on one of the lily ponds.

Amenities: Concierge, limited room service, valet parking, laundry, child care, children's program, four heated swimming pools, whirlpools, sauna, fitness center, four tennis courts, racquetball, croquet, water-sports rentals, gas grills, guest laundry, gift shops, full-service hair salon with massage and tanning.

MODERATE

Travelodge St. Pete Beach. 6300 Gulf Blvd. (at 63rd Ave.), St. Pete Beach, FL 33706. ☎ **800/237-8918** or 727/367-2711. Fax 727/367-7068. 200 units. A/C TV TEL. Winter $99–$141 double. Off-season $75–$129 double. AE, DC, DISC, MC, V.

The former Colonial Gateway Inn, this U-shaped beachfront complex of one- and two-story units is a favorite with families. All completely renovated in 1999, the rooms are contemporary, with light wood and beach tones. Most face the pool and a central landscaped courtyard, and about half are efficiencies with kitchenettes.

On the premises is a branch of the very good Shells seafood restaurant (see "Where to Dine," in chapter 1). An indoor lounge and a lively beach bar offer light refreshments. Facilities include an outdoor heated swimming pool with an expansive concrete deck, a kiddie pool, shuffleboard, and a game room. The water-sports shack here offers parasailing equipment rentals and also services the Days Inn Island Beach Resort next door (see above).

INEXPENSIVE

✪ **Beach Haven.** 4980 Gulf Blvd. (at 50th Ave.), St. Pete Beach, FL 33706. ☎ 727/367-8642. Fax 727/360-8202. www.beachhavenvillas.com. E-mail: jzpag@aol.com. 18 units. A/C TV TEL. Winter $75–$137 double. Off-season $52–$115 double. MC, V.

Nestled on the beach between two high-rise condos, these low-slung, pink-with-white-trim structures look from the outside like the early 1950s motel they once were. But Jone and Millard

Gamble (they also own the charming Island's End Resort, below) have replaced the innards and installed bright tile floors, vertical blinds, pastel tropical furniture, and many modern amenities, including TVs, VCRs, and refrigerators. Five of the original quarters remain as motel rooms (with shower-only bathrooms), but the Gambles linked the others to make 12 one-bedroom and one two-bedroom units. The top choice is the one-bedroom suite with sliding glass doors opening to a deck shaded by a sprawling Brazilian pepper tree. There's an outdoor heated pool surrounded by a white picket fence, plus a sunning deck with lounge furniture by the beach. You don't get maid service on Sunday or holidays, and the rooms and baths are 1950s smallish, but every unit here is bright, airy, and comfortable. Complimentary coffee and tea are served to all guests 2 days a week, and guests can use barbecue grills and a coin laundry. This is the heart of the hotel district, so lots of restaurants are just steps away.

Captain's Quarters Inn. 10035 Gulf Blvd. (between 100th and 101st aves.), Treasure Island, FL 33706. ☎ **800/526-9547** or 727/360-1659. Fax 727/363-3074. www.gulfcoastflorida.com/cqinn/. 9 units, including 1 cottage. A/C TV TEL. Winter $70–$100 double. Off-season $55–$75 double. Weekly rates available. MC, V. Small dogs accepted at extra charge.

Owned and operated by Britishers Nick and Deborah Russell, this nautically themed property offers well-kept accommodations on the gulf at inland rates. All but one of the units are huddled along 100 yards of beach, an ideal vantage point for sunset-watching. Six units are efficiencies (two of them on the beach) with mini-kitchens including microwave oven, coffeemaker, and wet bar or sink. There's also a bayside cottage with separate bedroom and a full kitchen. Facilities include an outdoor solar-heated freshwater swimming pool, a sundeck, guest barbecues, and a library.

✪ **Island's End Resort.** 1 Pass-a-Grille Way (at 1st Ave.), St. Pete Beach, FL 33706. ☎ **727/360-5023.** Fax 727/367-7890. www.islandsend.com. E-mail: jzgpag@aol.com. 6 units. A/C TV TEL. Dec 15 to June 1 $90–$185 cottage. Off-season $64–$185 cottage. Weekly rates available. MC, V.

A wonderful respite from the madding crowd, and a great bargain to boot, this little all-cottage hideaway sits right on the southern tip of St. Pete Beach, smack-dab on Pass-a-Grille, where the Gulf of Mexico meets Tampa Bay. You can step from the six contemporary cottages right onto the beach. And since the island curves sharply here, nothing blocks your view of the emerald bay. Strong currents run through the pass, however, but you can safely swim in the gulf or grab a brilliant sunset at the Pass-a-Grille public beach, just one door removed. Linked to each other by boardwalks, the comfortable one- or three-bedroom cottages have dining areas, living rooms, VCRs, and kitchens. You will love the one monstrous unit with two living rooms (one can be converted to sleeping quarters), two bathrooms (one with a whirlpool tub and separate shower), and its own private bayside swimming pool. You can meet your fellow guests at complimentary continental breakfasts served under a gazebo Tuesday, Thursday, and Saturday mornings (you can squeeze your own oranges). Facilities include a fishing dock, patios, decks, barbecues, and hammocks. Maid service is provided only upon request. Owners Jone and Millard Gamble are no fools: They live at this shady, idyllic setting.

INDIAN ROCKS BEACH AREA

Great Heron Inn. 68 Gulf Blvd. (south of 1st Ave.), Indian Rocks Beach, FL 33785. ☎ **727/595-2589.** Fax 727/596-7309. www.llc.net/~heroninn. E-mail: heroninn@llc.net. 16 units. A/C TV TEL. Winter $85–$88 double. Off-season $63–$68 double. Weekly and monthly rates available. DISC, MC, V. Hotel is 4 blocks south of Fla. 688.

A real heron named Harry patrols the beach at this family-oriented motel owned and operated by transplanted Michiganders Ralph and Teena Hickerson. It sits at the narrowest section of Indian Rocks Beach, facing the gulf on one side and its own Intracoastal Waterway dock on the other. The buildings flank a central courtyard, with a heated pool, which opens to the beach. The rooms offer modern furnishings and Berber carpets, and each unit has a full kitchen and dining area. Facilities include a coin-operated laundry, and picnic tables. There's a boat dock across the boulevard.

✪ **Pelican—East & West.** 108 21st Ave. (at Gulf Blvd.), Indian Rocks Beach, FL 33785. ☎ **727/595-9741.** Fax 727/596-4170. www.beachdirectory.com/pelican. E-mail: pelicanewmotel@aol.com. 8 units. A/C TV. Winter $50–$75 double. Off-season $45–$65 double. Weekly rates available. MC, V.

"PDIP" (Perfect Day in Paradise) is the motto at Mike and Carol McGlaughlin's motel complex, which offers a choice of two settings. Their lowest rates are at Pelican East, in a residential area 500 feet from the beach, where four suites each have a bedroom, a separate kitchen, and shower-only bathrooms. You'll pay more at Pelican West, but it's directly on the beachfront. The four beachside apartments each have a living room, bedroom, kitchen, patio, tub-shower combination bathrooms, and unbeatable views of the gulf. You won't get any frills here, such as phones in your rooms or a swimming pool, and the furniture is simple and dated. But this is a clean, comfortable, friendly choice. There's no restaurant on the premises, but Guppy's is 4 blocks away (see "Where to Dine," below).

CLEARWATER BEACH
MODERATE

Best Western Sea Stone Resort. 445 Hamden Dr. (at Coronado Dr.), Clearwater Beach, FL 33767. ☎ **800/444-1919**, 800/528-1234, or 727/441-1722. Fax 727/441-1680. www.seawake.com. 106 units. A/C TV TEL. Winter $89–$159 double. Off-season $69–$129 double. AE, DC, DISC, MC, V. Pets accepted at extra charge.

Located just across the street from the beach in Clearwater Beach's busy south end, the Sea Stone is a six-story building of classic Key West–style architecture containing 43 one-bedroom suites, each with a kitchenette and a living room. Their living room windows look across external walkways to the harbor. A few steps away, the older five-story Gulfview Wing offers 65 bedrooms. The furnishings are bright and airy, with pastel tones, light woods, and sea scenes on the walls. The on-site Marker 5 Restaurant serves breakfast only. There's valet laundry service, newspaper delivery, and complimentary coffee in the lobby. Facilities include a heated outdoor swimming pool, whirlpool, boat dock, coin laundry, and meeting rooms.

○ **Clearwater Beach Hotel.** 500 Mandalay Ave. (at Baymont St.), Clearwater Beach, FL 33767. ☎ **800/292-2295** or 727/441-2425. Fax 727/449-2083. www.clearwaterbeachhotel.com. E-mail: cbhotel@msn.com. 157 units. A/C TV TEL. Winter $159–$249 double. Off-season $115–$209 double. AE, DC, MC, V. Pets accepted at extra charge.

Besides the great beach location, you'll enjoy easy access to many nearby shops and restaurants from this Old Florida–style structure, built in the 1970s to replace an old wooden hotel. It's been owned and operated by the same family since the 1950s and attracts an older clientele and some families. Directly on the gulf, the complex consists of a six-story main building and two-story motel-style wings. Rooms and rates vary according to location— bay view or gulf view, poolside or beachfront. Some rooms have balconies. The formal dining room is romantic at sunset and offers great views of the gulf, while the nautically themed lounge has entertainment nightly. A bar provides snacks and libations beside an outdoor heated swimming pool. There's limited room service, valet laundry service, and free valet parking.

Palm Pavilion Inn. 18 Bay Esplanade (at Mandalay Ave.), Clearwater Beach, FL 33767. ☎ **800/433-PALM** or 727/446-6777. Fax 727/461-0355. www. palmpavilioninn.com. 28 units. A/C TV TEL. Winter $87–$125 double. Off-season $59–$89 double. AE, DISC, MC, V.

Just north of the tourist area, this three-story walk-up beachfront spot is removed from the bustle yet within easy walking distance of all the action. The three-story art deco building is artfully trimmed in peach and teal. The lobby area and guest rooms, also art deco in design, feature rounded light wood and rattan furnishings, sea-toned fabrics, photographs from the 1920s to 1950s era, and vertical blinds. Entered from internal corridors (no balconies or patios here), rooms in the west side of the house face the gulf, while those in the east face the bay. Three efficiencies have kitchenettes. Facilities include a rooftop sundeck, heated swimming pool, complimentary coffee, and beach chair and umbrella rentals. By the beach, the Palm Pavilion Grill & Bar is a fine place to catch the sunset and some live entertainment Tuesday to Sunday nights during winter, on weekends off-season. Lighted tennis courts and an athletic center are across the street.

Radisson Suite Resort on Sand Key. 1201 Gulf Blvd., Clearwater Beach, FL 33767. ☎ **800/333-3333** or 727/596-1100. Fax 727/595-4292. www. radissonsandkey.com. E-mail: reservations@radissonsandkey.com. 220 units. A/C MINIBAR TV TEL. $139–$299 suite. Packages available. AE, DC, DISC, MC, V.

You'll see the beauty of Sand Key from the suites in this boomerang-shaped, 10-story hotel overlooking Clearwater Bay. The gulf is just beyond a row of high-rise condos across the street, and beautiful Sand Key Park is a few steps away. The whole family will enjoy exploring the adjacent boardwalk with 25 shops and restaurants. Each suite has a bedroom with a balcony offering water views, as well as a complete living room with a sofa bed, wet bar, entertainment unit, coffeemaker, and microwave oven. Like the Sheraton Sand Key across the boulevard (see below), this Radisson gets many European guests during the summer months, so there's negligible fluctuation in room rates during the year.

The Harbor Grille offers fresh seafood, steaks, and grand bay views. The Harbor Lounge has live entertainment. In a clapboard, shingle-roof building out by the pool, Kokomo's serves light fare and tropical drinks. Other amenities here include limited room service, laundry, free trolley to the beach, year-round children's activities program, free valet parking, masseuse, bay-side outdoor heated swimming pool with rock waterfall and bar, sundeck, sauna, exercise room, guest laundry, waterfront boardwalk with a variety of shops and restaurants.

✪ **Sheraton Sand Key Resort.** 1160 Gulf Blvd., Clearwater Beach, FL 33767. ☎ **800/325-3535** or 727/595-1611. Fax 727/596-8488. www. beachsand.com. E-mail: sheraton@cft.net. 390 units. A/C TV TEL. Winter $170–$220 double. Off-season $109 –$170 double. AE, DC, DISC, MC, V.

Away from the honky-tonk of Clearwater, this nine-story Spanish-look hotel on 10 acres next to Sand Key Park is a big favorite with water-sports enthusiasts and groups. It also gets lots of European guests year-round. The guest rooms here all have dark-wood furniture, coffeemakers, hair dryers, and a balcony or patio with views of the gulf or the bay.

Rusty's Restaurant serves breakfast and dinner; for lighter fare, try the Island Café, the Sundeck, or Fast Johnny's Poolside Snack Bar out by an attractive pool area by the beach. The Snack Store is open 24 hours.

Amenities include limited room service, newspaper delivery, in-room massage, valet parking and laundry, child care, children's program (summer only), beachside outdoor heated swimming pool, fitness center, whirlpool, three lighted tennis courts, beach volleyball, newsstand, game room, children's pool, playground, water-sports rentals, 24-hour general store.

INEXPENSIVE

✪ **Sun West Beach Motel.** 409 Hamden Dr. (at Bayside Dr.), Clearwater Beach, FL 33767. ☎ **727/442-5008.** Fax 727/461-1395. www.clearwaterbeach. com/sunwest/sunwest.html. E-mail: sunwest1@gte.net. 15 units. A/C TV TEL. $42–$60 double; $50–$80 efficiency, $68–$145 suite. MC, V.

Sitting among several small motels a 2-block walk from the beach, Scott and Judy Barrows' one-story establishment dates from 1954, but it's well maintained, overlooks the bay, and has fishing/boating dock, a heated bayside pool and sundeck, a shuffleboard court, and guest laundry. All units, which face either the bay, the pool, or the sundeck, were recently upgraded and have tropical-style furnishings. The four motel rooms have small refrigerators, the 10 efficiencies have kitchens, and a few suites have separate bedrooms. The biggest and best unit is the Bayside Suite, which has vaulted ceilings, a steam room in its bathroom, and a fully equipped kitchen.

TWO NEARBY GOLF RESORTS

Belleview Biltmore Resort & Spa. 25 Belleview Blvd. (P.O. Box 2317), Clearwater, FL 33757. ☎ **800/237-8947** or 727/442-6171. Fax 727/441-4173 or 727/443-6361. 240 units. A/C MINIBAR TV TEL. Winter $159 double; $230–$310 suite. Off-season $109 double; $159–$229 suite. AE, DC, DISC, MC, V. Resort is 1 mile south of downtown on Belleview Rd., off Alt. U.S. 19.

As the Gulf Coast's oldest operating tourist hotel, this gabled clapboard structure was built in 1896 by Henry B. Plant as the Hotel Belleview to attract customers to his Orange Belt Railroad. On a bluff overlooking the bay, it's the largest occupied wooden structure in the world. Today it attracts mostly groups and serious golfers (guests can play at the adjoining Belleview Country Club, an 18-hole par-72 championship course), but there's no denying its Victorian charm and old-fashioned ambience—once you get past the out-of-place, glass-and-steel foyer added by more recent owners. Historic tours are given daily at 11am ($5 for adults, $3 for children 13 to 17, free for hotel guests and kids under 17). The creaky hallways lead to several shops and a museum explaining the hotel's history. Large, high-ceilinged guest rooms are decorated in Queen Anne style, with dark-wood period furniture.

The informal indoor/outdoor Terrace Café provides breakfast, lunch, or dinner. There's also a pub in the basement, a lounge, and a poolside bar. Amenities include limited room service, dry cleaning and valet laundry, nightly turndown on request, currency exchange, and child care; four red-clay tennis courts; indoor and outdoor heated swimming pools (one with a waterfall); whirlpool; spa with sauna; Swiss showers; workout gym; jogging and walking trails; bicycle rentals; yacht charters; gift shops; newsstand; and golf privileges at the country club.

✪ **The Westin Innisbrook Resort.** 36750 U.S. 19 North, Palm Harbor, FL 34684. ☎ **800/456-2000** or 727/942-2000. Fax 727/942-5577. www. westin-innisbrook.com. 800 units. A/C TV TEL. Winter $230–$455 double. Off-season $135–$375 double. Golf packages available. AE, DC, DISC, MC, V.

Golf Digest, Golf magazine, and others pick this as one of the country's best places to play (provided you stay here, of course). Situated off U.S. 19 between Palm Harbor and Tarpon Springs, this 1,000-acre resort has 90 holes on championship courses that are more like the rolling links of the Carolinas than the usually flat courses found in Florida. Innisbrook has the largest resort-owned and -operated golf school in North America. The resort also boasts 11 clay and 4 hard tennis courts. There's even a children's program to take care of the kids. The spacious quarters actually are privately owned homes and apartments spread all over the premises, so there are no focal points here except the building where you check in and the golf and tennis clubhouses.

8 Where to Dine

St. Pete Beach and Clearwater Beach both have a wide selection of national chain fast-food and family restaurants along their main drags.

As with the accommodations above, I have grouped the restaurants by geographic area: St. Pete Beach, including Pass-a-Grille; Indian Rocks Beach, including Madeira Beach, Redington Beach, North Redington Beach, Redington Shores, and Indian Shores; and finally, Clearwater Beach.

ST. PETE BEACH AREA

✪ **Crabby Bill's.** 5100 Gulf Blvd. (at 51st Ave.), St. Pete Beach. ☎ **727/ 360-8858.** Reservations not accepted. Sandwiches $4–$6; main courses $6–$22. AE, MC, V. Mon–Thurs 11:30am–10pm, Fri–Sat 11:30am–11pm, Sun noon–10pm. SEAFOOD.

The least expensive gulf-side dining here, this member of a small local chain sits right on the beach in the heart of the hotel district. There's an open-air rooftop bar, but big glass windows enclose the large dining room. They offer fine water views from picnic tables equipped with rolls of paper towels and buckets of saltine crackers, the better to eat the Alaskan, snow, and stone crabs that are the big draws here. The crustaceans fall into the moderate price category, but most other main courses, such as fried clam strips or a combo broiled fish platter, are inexpensive. The creamy smoked fish spread is a delicious appetizer, and you'll get enough to whet the appetites of at least two persons.

Hurricane. 807 Gulf Way (at 9th Ave.), Pass-a-Grille. ☎ **727/360-9558.** Reservations not accepted. Salads and sandwiches $2.50–$7; main courses $10–$17. AE, MC, V. Daily 8am–1am; breakfast Mon–Fri 8–11am, Sat–Sun 8am–noon. SEAFOOD.

A longtime institution across the street from Pass-a-Grille Public Beach, this three-level gray Victorian building with white gingerbread trim is a great place to toast the sunset, especially at the rooftop bar. It's more beach pub than fine restaurant, but the grouper sandwiches are excellent, and there's always fresh fish to be fried, broiled, or blackened, and shrimp and crab to be steamed. Downstairs you can dine inside the knotty-pine paneled dining room or on the sidewalk terrace, where bathers from across Gulf Way are welcome (there's a walk-up bar for beach libation). The second floor dining area also has seating on a wrap-around veranda. You must be at least 21 years old to go up to the Hurricane Watch rooftop bar or to join the revelry when the second level turns into Stormy's Nightclub at 10pm Tuesday to Saturday.

Internet Outpost Cafe. 7400 Gulf Blvd. (at Corey Ave./75th Ave.), St. Pete Beach. ☎ **727/360-7806.** Reservations not accepted. Coffee and pastries $1–$3; sandwiches $5–$6. AE, MC, V. Mon–Thurs 10am–10pm, Fri–Sat 10am–midnight. PASTRIES/SANDWICHES.

If you left your laptop at home and can't stand not getting your e-mail or surfing the Net, head for this cozy coffee emporium with nine computer terminals, all with fast connections to the Internet ($2 for 15 minutes access time). You can also lounge on the sofas and wing chairs while sipping your latte, kill a rainy afternoon playing chess, or listen to live music on Friday and Saturday evenings during summer. In addition to coffees, teas, and pastries available all hours, the lunch fare (11am to 2pm) includes freshly made chicken salad, Cuban, spicy turkey, and other sandwiches.

✪ **Skidder's Restaurant.** 5799 Gulf Blvd. (at 60th Ave.), St. Pete Beach. ☎ **727/360-1029.** Reservations accepted. Breakfast $3–$6; sandwiches and burgers $3.50–$8; pizza $6–$16; main courses $8–$15. AE, DC, DISC, MC, V. Daily 7am–11pm. ITALIAN/GREEK/AMERICAN.

A local favorite, this inexpensive family restaurant in the hotel district offers a full range of breakfast fare plus pizzas (available to eat here or carry out), burgers and sandwiches, big salads, gyro and souvlaki platters, and Italian-style veal and chicken dishes (sautéed in wine with artichokes is a house specialty). A children's menu features burgers and spaghetti.

INDIAN ROCKS BEACH AREA

You'll find a bay-front edition of **Shells,** the fine and inexpensive local seafood chain, opposite the Lobster Pot on Gulf Boulevard at 178th Avenue in Redington Shores (☎ **813/393-8990**). See "Where to Dine," in chapter 2, for more information about Shells' menu and prices, which are the same at all branches.

⭐ **Beachside Grille.** 35 182nd Ave. (at Gulf Blvd., opposite Friendly Tavern), Redington Shores. ☎ **727/397-1865.** Reservations not accepted. Sandwiches and burgers $5–$7.50; main courses $9–$15. AE, DISC, MC, V. Daily 11am–10pm. Closed Thanksgiving and Christmas. SEAFOOD.

Locals don't mind waiting for the best seafood bargains on the beach at this tiny (seven tables) place tucked into the rear of a two-story commercial building opposite the Friendly Tavern, a major landmark in Redington Shores. They are rewarded with a savory Louisiana seafood gumbo as a starter, then off-the-boat-fresh grouper or mahimahi, grilled or blackened, salmon under a dill sauce, or grilled shrimp with a zesty fruit salsa. Falling-off-the-bone barbecued ribs, chargrilled steaks, and steamed shrimp and crab legs also appear on the menu. Main courses come with rice, sauteed vegetables, and a salad with owner Dan Casey's pesto salad dressing, which is so good he sells it by the bottle. Try a pitcher of the homemade white or red sangria, another local favorite. The lunch menu features hot dogs with french fries, stuffed pitas, and subs and other sandwiches.

⭐ **Guppy's.** 1701 Gulf Blvd. (at 17th St.), Indian Rocks Beach. ☎ **813/593-2032.** Reservations not accepted. Sandwiches $5.50–$9; main courses $9–$16. AE, DC, DISC, MC, V. Sun–Thurs 11:30am–10:30pm; Fri–Sat 11:30am–11pm. SEAFOOD.

Locals also love this small bar and grill across from Indian Rocks Public Beach because they know they'll always get terrific chow (it's associated with the excellent Lobster Pot, mentioned below). You won't soon forget the salmon coated with potatoes and lightly fried, then baked with a creamy leek and garlic sauce; it's fattening, yes, but also a bargain at $9. Another good choice is lightly cooked tuna finished with a peppercorn sauce. The atmosphere is casual beach friendly, with a fun bar in the rear. Scotty's famous upside-down apple-walnut pie topped with ice cream will require a little extra work on the weights tomorrow. You can dine outside on a patio beside the main road.

⭐ **Lobster Pot.** 17814 Gulf Blvd. (at 178th Ave.), Redington Shores. ☎ **727/391-8592.** Reservations recommended. Main courses $14.50–$29.50. AE, DC, MC, V. Mon–Thurs 4:30–10pm, Fri–Sat 4:30–11pm, Sun 4–10pm. SEAFOOD.

Step into this weathered-looking restaurant near the beach and owner Eugen Fuhrmann will tell you to get ready to experience the finest seafood in the area. The prices are high, but the variety of Maine lobster dishes is amazing. The lobster américaine is flambéed in brandy with garlic, and the bouillabaisse is as authentic as any you'd find in the south of France. In addition to lobster, there's a wide selection of grouper, snapper, salmon, swordfish, shrimp, scallops, crab, and Dover sole, most prepared with elaborate sauces. There's no ordinary children's menu here: It features half a Maine lobster and a petite filet mignon.

✪ **The Salt Rock Grill.** 19325 Gulf Blvd. (north of 193rd Ave.), Indian Shores. ☎ **727/593-7625.** Reservations recommended. Main courses $12–$34 (early bird specials $8–$10). AE, DC, DISC, MC, V. Sun–Thurs 4–10pm, Fri–Sat 4–11pm (early bird specials daily 4–5:30pm). SEAFOOOD/STEAKS.

Affluent professionals and other gorgeous folk always pack this waterfront restaurant, making it *the* place to see and be seen on the beaches. The big, urbane dining room is built on three levels, thus affording every table a view over the creeklike waterway out back. And in warm, fair weather you can dine out by the dock or slake your thirst at the lively tiki bar (bands play out here on Sundays during the summer). Anything from the wood-fired grill is excellent here. Thick, aged steaks are the house specialties, as are crusted rack of lamb and Havana-style pork tenderloin. You can get a good sampling with the mixed grill: small portions of filet mignon, pork tenderloin, Jamaican jerk chicken breast, a two-bone lamb chop, and dessert-sweet coconut shrimp. Pan-seared peppered tuna and salmon cooked on a cedar board lead the seafood.

CLEARWATER BEACH

Bob Heilman's Beachcomber. 447 Mandalay Ave. (at Papaya St.). ☎ **727/442-4144.** Reservations recommended. Main courses $12–$29. AE, DC, DISC, MC, V. Mon–Sat 11:30am–11pm, Sun noon–10pm. AMERICAN.

In a row of restaurants, bars, and T-shirt shops, Bob and Sherri Heilman's establishment has been popular with the locals since 1948. Each dining room here has its own special theme: large model sailing crafts making one seem nautical, a pianist making music in a second, works of art creating a gallery in a third, and booths and a fireplace making for a cozy fourth. The menu presents a variety of fresh seafood, beef, veal, and lamb selections. If you tire of fruits-of-the-sea, the "back-to-the-farm" fried chicken—from an original 1910 Heilman family recipe—is incredible. The Beachcomber shares an extensive wine collection with Bobby's Bistro & Wine Bar (see below).

Bobby's Bistro & Wine Bar. 447 Mandalay Ave. (at Papaya St., behind Bob Heilman's Beachcomber). ☎ **727/446-9463.** Reservations not accepted. Sandwiches and pizzas $6–$10; main courses $10–$16. AE, DC, DISC, MC, V. Sun–Thurs 5pm–11pm, Fri–Sat 5pm–midnight. AMERICAN.

Son of Bob Heilman's Beachcomber, this bistro draws a more urbane crowd that its parent. A wine-cellar theme is amply justified by the real thing: a walk-in closet with several thousand bottles kept at a constant 55°F. Walk through and pick your vintage, then listen to jazz while you dine inside at tall, bar-height tables or outside on a covered patio. The chef specializes in gourmet pizzas on homemade focaccia crust (as a tasty appetizer), plus charcoal-grilled veal chops, filet mignon, fresh fish, and monstrous pork chops with caramelized Granny Smith apples and a Mount Vernon mustard sauce. Everything's served à la carte here, so watch your credit card. On the other hand, there's an affordable sandwich menu featuring the likes of bronzed grouper and chicken with a spicy Jack cheese.

Frenchy's Cafe. 41 Baymont St. ☎ **727/446-3607.** Reservations not accepted. Sandwiches and burgers $4–$7. AE, MC, V. Mon–Thurs 11:30am–11pm, Fri–Sat 11:30am–midnight, Sun noon–11pm. SEAFOOD.

Always popular with locals and visitors in the know, this casual pub makes the best grouper sandwiches in the area and has all the awards to prove it. They're fresh, thick, juicy, and delicious. The atmosphere is pure Florida casual style. There's usually a wait during the winter and on weekends all year.

For more casual fare directly on the beach, **Frenchy's Rockaway Grill,** at 7 Rockaway St. (☎ **727/446-4844**), has a wonderful outdoor setting.

✪ **Seafood & Sunsets at Julie's.** 351 S. Gulfview Blvd. (at 5th St.), Clearwater Beach. ☎ **727/441-2548.** Reservations not accepted. Salads and sandwiches $5–$8; main courses $8–$22. AE, MC, V. Daily 11am–10pm. SEAFOOD.

A Key West–style tradition takes over Julie Nichols' place at dusk as both locals and visitors gather at sidewalk tables or in the tiny, rustic upstairs bar to toast the sunset over the beach across the street. The predominately seafood menu features fine renditions of charcoal-broiled mahimahi with sour cream, Parmesan and herb sauce; bacon-wrapped barbecued shrimp on a skewer; broiled, fried, or blackened fresh Florida grouper; and flounder stuffed with crabmeat. Everything is cooked to order here, so come prepared to linger over a cold drink.

9   The Beaches After Dark

If you haven't already found it during your sightseeing and shop-ping excursions, the restored fishing community of **John's Pass Village and Boardwalk,** on Gulf Boulevard at John's Pass in Madeira Beach, has plenty of restaurants, bars, and shops to keep you occupied after the sun sets. Elsewhere, the nightlife scene at the beach revolves around rocking bars that pump out the music until 2am.

Down south in Pass-a-Grille, there's the popular, always lively lounge in **Hurricane,** on Gulf Way at 9th Avenue opposite the public beach (see "Where to Dine," above).

On Treasure Island, **Beach Nutts,** on West Gulf Boulevard at 96th Ave. (☎ 727/367-7427), is perched atop a stilt foundation like a wooden beach cottage on the Gulf of Mexico. The music ranges from Top 40 to reggae and rock. Up on the northern tip of Treasure Island, **Gators on the Pass** (☎ 727/367-8951) claims to have the world's longest waterfront bar, with a huge deck overlooking the waters of John's Pass. The complex also includes a no-smoking sports bar and a three-story tower with a top-level observation deck for panoramic views of the Gulf of Mexico. There's live music, from acoustic and blues to rock, most nights.

In Clearwater Beach, the **Palm Pavilion Grill & Bar,** on the beach at 18 Bay Esplanade (☎ 727/446-6777), has live music Tuesday through Sunday nights during the winter, on weekends off-season. Nearby, **Frenchy's Rockaway Grill,** at 7 Rockaway St. (☎ 727/446-4844), is another popular hangout.

If you're into laughs, **Coconuts Comedy Club,** at the Howard Johnson motel, Gulf Boulevard at 61st Avenue in St. Pete Beach (☎ 727/360-5653), has an ever-changing program of live stand-up funny men and women. Call for the schedule, performers, and prices.

For a more highbrow evening, go to the Clearwater mainland and the 2,200-seat **Ruth Eckerd Hall,** 1111 McMullen-Booth Rd. (☎ 727/791-7400; www.rutheckerdhall.com), which hosts a varied program of Broadway shows, ballet, drama, symphonic works, popular music, jazz, and country music.

10 An Excursion to Tarpon Springs

One of Florida's most fascinating small towns and a fine day trip from Tampa, St. Petersburg, or the beaches, Tarpon Springs calls itself the "Sponge Capital of the World." That's because Greek immigrants from the Dodecanese Islands settled here in the late 19th century to harvest sponges, which grew in abundance off-shore. By the 1930s, Tarpon Springs was producing more sponges than any other place in the world. A blight ruined the business in the 1940s, but the descendants of those early immigrants stayed on. Today they comprise about a third of the population, making Tarpon Springs a center of transplanted Greek culture.

Although sponges still arrive at the historic Sponge Docks on Dodecanese Boulevard, the town's mainstays today are commercial fishing and tourism. With a lively, carnival-like atmosphere, the docks are a great place to spend an afternoon or early evening, poking your head into shops selling sponges and other souvenirs while Greek music comes from the dozen or so family restaurants purveying authentic Aegean cuisine. You can also venture off-shore from here, for booths on the docks hawk sightseeing and fishing cruises.

Just south of the docks, restored Victorian homes facing the winding creek known as Spring Bayou make this one of the most picturesque towns in the state.

ESSENTIALS

From Tampa or St. Petersburg, take U.S. 19 north and turn left on Tarpon Avenue (County Road 582). From Clearwater Beach, take Alt. U.S. 19 north through Dunedin. The center of the historic downtown district is at the intersection of Pinellas Avenue (Alt. U.S. 19) and Tarpon Avenue. To reach the Sponge Docks, go 10 blocks north on Pinellas Avenue and turn left at Pappas' Restaurant onto Dodecanese Boulevard.

The **Tarpon Springs Chamber of Commerce,** 11 E. Orange St., Tarpon Springs, FL 34689 (☎ **727/937-6109;** fax 727/937-2879; www.tarponsprings.com), has an information office on Dodecanese Boulevard at the Sponge Docks. Open Tuesday to Saturday from 10:30am to 4:30pm, Sunday from 11am to 5pm.

EXPLORING THE TOWN

Two areas are worth visiting here. You'll first come to the **Tarpon Springs Downtown Historic District,** with its turn-of-the-century commercial buildings along Tarpon Avenue and Pinellas Avenue (Alt. U.S. 19). The **Tarpon Springs Cultural Center,** on Pinellas Avenue a block south of Tarpon Avenue, explains the town's history and has visitor information. On Tarpon Avenue west of Pinellas Avenue, you'll come to the Victorian homes overlooking **Spring Bayou.** This creekside area makes for a delightfully picturesque stroll.

The carnival-like **Sponge Docks** run alongside Dodecanese Boulevard, which is peppered with shops, restaurants, and fishing-and sightseeing boats pulling at their mooring lines along the riverside boardwalk. Poke your head into the tin-roofed **Sponge-orama** (no phone), a museum dedicated to sponges and sponge divers. You can buy a wide variety of sponges here (they'll ship them home) and watch a 30-minute video about sponge diving several times a day. Admission is free. The Spongeorama is open daily from 10am to 5pm. In the **Coral Sea Aquarium,** at the western end of the boulevard (☎ 727/938-5378), a scuba diver feeds sharks at 11:30am and 1, 2:30, and 4pm. The aquarium is open daily from 10am to 5pm. Admission is $4.75 adults, $4 seniors, $2.75 for children 3 to 11, free for kids under 3.

You also can go on sightseeing, lunch, or sunset cruises down the Anclote River with **Island Cruises** (☎ 727/934-0606); spend 30 minutes watching the sponge divers at work with **St. Nicolas Boat Line** (☎ 727/942-6425); or try your luck out in the gulf on a party boat operated by **Dolphin Deep Sea Fishing** (☎ 727/937-8257). Booths along the docks sell tickets for these and other excursions. Make your reservations as soon as you get here, then go sightseeing ashore while you wait for the next boat to shove off.

Bikers, in-line skaters, hikers, and joggers can come right through downtown on the **Pinellas Trail,** which runs along Safford Avenue and crosses Tarpon Avenue 2 blocks east of Pinellas Avenue (see "Outdoor Pursuits & Spectator Sports" in chapter 3).

WHERE TO DINE

Your Tarpon Springs experience will be incomplete without taking a Greek meal here. In addition to Hellas Restaurant & Bakery listed below, you'll find about a dozen other family-owned restaurants along the lively Sponge Docks, all of them clean, inviting, and serving authentic, inexpensive Greek fare.

Weight-watchers should studiously avoid the **Parthenon Bakery & Pastry Shop**, 751 Dodecanese Blvd. (☎ **727/ 938-7709**), where huge cabinets are filled with Greek and other delights, including luscious chocolate-covered baklava. Open daily 9am to 10pm.

✪ **Hellas Restaurant & Bakery.** Sponge Docks, 785 Dodecanese Blvd. ☎ **727/943-2400.** Reservations accepted. Sandwiches and salads $4–$6; main courses $7.50–$14. AE, DC, DISC, MC, V. Daily 11am–10pm. GREEK.

The lovely hand-painted tile tables on the street-side patio here make fine spots from which to watch the action on the Sponge Docks while sampling authentic Aegean cuisine. If you like feta cheese, you'll enjoy the pungent Greek-style shrimp or scallops. If not, opt for the perfectly pan-fried grouper or any of the Aegean standbys: moussaka, pastisio, dolmades, or one of the largest gyro sandwiches in town (you can try a little of each on the sampler platter). The bakery supplies baklava, galactombouriko (egg custard), and other desserts from the old country. With Greek cuisine, Greek music, and a Greek-looking (if not Greek-accented) waiter, it's easy to imagine yourself quayside on Mykonos.

Louis Pappas' Restaurant and Riverside Cafe. Sponge Docks, 10 Dodecanese Blvd. (at Pinellas Ave./Alt. U.S. 19). ☎ **727/937-5101.** Reservations accepted. Sandwiches and tapas $6–$8; main courses $10–$18. AE, MC, V. Sun–Thurs 11:30am–10pm, Fri–Sat 11:30am–11pm (bar closes 1 hour later). GREEK/SEAFOOD.

The most upscale restaurant here, Pappas' is famous statewide for its fresh Greek- and American-style seafood—shrimp, grouper, red snapper, and even stone crab claws in season—most of it right off the boat. There are also Greek salads and other dishes with an Aegean flair, such as salmon with a Greek-seasoned stuffing. The family-run restaurant has been operating on the banks of the Anclote River since 1925 when it was founded by Louis Pappamichaelopoulus of Sparta, Greece. The bar area doubles as the Riverside Cafe, serving a light menu of sandwiches and tapas. You get nice river views from the tall windows of this modern building. Downstairs, you can poke through several shops, including one selling hand-rolled cigars.

5

Sarasota

*F*ar enough away from Tampa Bay to have an identity very much its own, Sarasota is one of Florida's cultural centers. In fact, many retirees spend their winters here because there's so much to keep them entertained and stimulated, including the very fine Asolo Center for the Performing Arts and the Van Wezel Performing Arts Hall. Like affluent Naples down in Southwest Florida, it also has an extensive array of first-class resorts, restaurants, and upscale boutiques.

Offshore, 35 miles of gloriously white beaches fringe a chain of long, narrow barrier islands. Shielded from the gulf by **Lido Key,** which has a string of affordable hotels attractive to family vacationers, **St. Armands Key** sports one of Florida's ritziest shopping and dining districts. To the south, **Siesta Key** is a quiet residential enclave popular with artisans and writers but also home to Siesta Village, this area's funky, laid-back, and often noisy beach hangout. And stretching north to Bradenton, **Longboat Key** is one of Florida's wealthiest islands.

Legend has it that Sarasota was named after the explorer Hernando de Soto's daughter, Sara (hence, Sara-sota). In more recent times, the town's most famous resident was circus legend John Ringling, who came here in the 1920s.

Ringling built a palatial bay-front mansion known as Ca'd'Zan, acquired extensive real estate holdings, erected a magnificent museum to house his world-class collection of baroque paintings, and built the causeway out to St. Armands and Lido keys.

Sarasota is only 10 miles south of Bradenton (see section 6, below), and the two share an airport, which sits astride their mutual boundary halfway between the two downtowns. Accordingly, you can stay in either town and easily explore the other.

1   Orientation

ARRIVING

You probably will get a less expensive airfare by flying into **Tampa International Airport,** an hour's drive north of Sarasota (see "Getting There & Getting Around" in chapter 1), and you could save even more since Tampa's rental-car agencies often offer some of the best deals in Florida. If you decide to fly directly here, **Sarasota-Bradenton International Airport** (☎ **941/359-2770**), north of downtown off University Parkway between U.S. 41 and U.S. 301, is served by **American** (☎ 800/433-7300), **America Trans Air** (☎ 800/225-2995), **Canada 3000** (☎ 800/993-4378), **Continental** (☎ 800/525-0280), **Delta** (☎ 800/221-1212), **Northwest/KLM** (☎ 800/225-2525), **TWA** (☎ 800/221-2000), and **US Airways** (☎ 800/428-4322).

Alamo (☎ 800/327-9633), **Avis** (☎ 800/331-1212), **Budget** (☎ 800/527-0700), **Dollar** (☎ 800/800-4000), **Enterprise** (☎ 800/325-8007), **Hertz** (☎ 800/654-3131), and **National** (☎ 800/CAR-RENT) have car rentals here.

Diplomat Taxi (☎ **941/355-5155**) has a monopoly on service from the airport to hotels in Sarasota and Bradenton. Look for the cabs at the west end of the terminal outside baggage claim. The fare is about $9 to downtown Sarasota, $10 to $15 to St. Armands and Lido keys, $14 to $23 to Siesta Key, and $14 to $32 to Longboat Key.

Amtrak has bus connections to its Tampa station (☎ **800/USA-RAIL**).

VISITOR INFORMATION

Contact the **Sarasota Convention and Visitors Bureau,** 655 N. Tamiami Trail (U.S. 41), Sarasota, FL 34236 (☎ **800/522-9799** or 941/957-1877; fax 941/951-2956; www.sarasotafl.org). The bureau and its helpful visitors center are in a blue pagoda-shaped building on Tamiami Trail (U.S. 41) at 6th Street. They're open Monday to Saturday from 9am to 5pm, Sunday from 11am to 3pm. Closed holidays.

For information specific to the keys, contact the **Siesta Key Chamber of Commerce,** 5100-B Ocean Blvd., Sarasota, FL 34242 (☎ **941/349-3800;** fax 941/349-9699; www.siestakeychamber.com; e-mail: skchamber@msn.com), or the **Longboat Key**

Sarasota & Bradenton

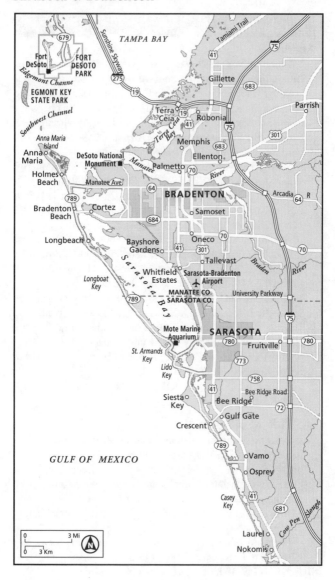

Chamber of Commerce, 6854 Gulf of Mexico Dr., Longboat Key, FL (☎ **941/383-2646;** fax 941/383-8217; www. longboatkeychamber.com).

2 Getting Around

Sarasota County Area Transit (SCAT) (☎ **941/316-1234**) provides regularly scheduled bus service. The Sarasota Convention and Visitors Bureau distributes route maps (see "Visitor Information," above).

Taxi companies include **Diplomat Taxi** (☎ **941/355-5155**), **Green Cab Taxi** (☎ **941/922-6666**), and **Yellow Cab of Sarasota** (☎ **941/955-3341**).

3 Hitting the Beach

Much of the area's 35 miles of beaches are occupied by hotels and condominium complexes, but there are excellent public beaches here. The area's most popular beach is **Siesta Key Public Beach,** with a picnic area, 700-car parking lot, crowds of families, and quartz sand reminiscent of the blazingly white beaches in Northwest Florida. There's also beach access at **Siesta Village,** which has a plethora of casual restaurants and pubs with outdoor seating (see "Where to Dine," below). More secluded and quiet is **Turtle Beach,** at Siesta Key's south end. It has shelters, boat ramps, picnic tables, and volleyball nets.

After you've driven the length of Longboat Key and admired the luxurious homes and condos blocking access to the beach, take a right off St. Armands Circle onto Lido Key and **North Lido Beach.** The south end of the island is occupied by **South Lido Beach Park,** with plenty of shade making it a good spot for picnics and walks.

4 Outdoor Pursuits & Spectator Sports

BICYCLING & IN-LINE SKATING

You can bike and skate from downtown to Lido and Longboat keys, since paved walkways/bike paths run alongside the John Ringling Causeway and then up Longboat. You can rent bikes and blades at **C.B.'s Saltwater Outfitters,** 1249 Stickney Point Rd., at the Siesta Key side of the Stickney Point Bridge (☎ **941/ 349-4400**), and at **Siesta Sports Rentals,** 6551 Midnight Pass Rd., in the Southbridge Mall just south of Stickney Point Bridge on Siesta Key (☎ **941/346-1797**), has bikes of various sizes, including stroller attachments for kids, plus motor scooters. Bike rentals range from about $14 a day to $45 a week.

BOAT RENTALS

All Watersports, in the Boatyard Shopping Village, on the mainland end of Stickney Point Bridge (☎ **941/921-2754**), rents personal watercraft such as Wave Runners, jet boats, and jet-skis, as well as speedboats, runabouts, and bowriders. At the island end of the bridge, **C.B.'s Saltwater Outfitters,** 1249 Stickney Point Rd. (☎ **941/349-4400**), and **Siesta Key Boat Rentals,** 1265 Old Stickney Point Rd. (☎ **941/349-8880**), both rent runabouts, pontoon boats, and other craft. Bait and tackle are available at the marinas.

CRUISES

The area's best nature cruises go forth from Mote Marine Aquarium (see "Parks, Nature Preserves & Gardens," below).

From October to May, you can head over to **Marina Jack,** U.S. 41 at Island Park Circle, for 2-hour sightseeing and sunset cruises around Sarasota's waterways aboard the 65-foot, two-deck *Le Barge* (☎ **941/366-6116**). The cruises run Tuesday to Sunday, with the sightseeing cruise leaving at 2pm. The sunset cruises with live music change with the time of sunset. The cruises cost $15 adults, $5 for kids under 13. Snacks and libation are available for an extra charge. Call for reservations.

FISHING

Charter fishing boats dock at most marinas here. The **Flying Fish Fleet**, downtown at Marina Jack's Marina, U.S. 41 at Island Park Circle (☎ **941/366-3373**), offers party boat charter-fishing excursions, with bait and tackle furnished. Prices for half-day trips are $28 adults, $23 seniors, $18 for kids 4 to 12. All-day voyages cost $40, $35, and $30, respectively. Call for the schedule. Charter boats also line up along the dock here.

GOLF

The **Bobby Jones Golf Complex,** 1000 Circus Blvd. (☎ **941/ 365-GOLF**), is Sarasota's only municipal facility, but it has two 18-hole championship layouts—the American (par 71) and

British (par 72) courses—and the 9-hole Gillespie executive course (par 30). Tee times are assigned 3 days in advance. Greens fees range from $25 to $31, including cart rental.

You can also tune your game at the public **Village Green Golf Club,** 3500 Pembroke Dr., near Bee Ridge and Beneva roads (☎ **941/925-2755**), whose executive-length 18 holes can be parred in 58.

The semiprivate **Rolling Green Golf Club,** 4501 Tuttle Ave. (☎ **941/355-6620**), is an 18-hole, par-72 course. Facilities include a driving range, rental clubs, and lessons. Tee times are assigned 2 days in advance. Prices, including cart, are about $40 in winter, $25 off-season.

Also semiprivate, the **Sarasota Golf Club,** 7820 N. Leewynn Dr. (☎ **941/371-2431**), is an 18-hole, par-72 course. Facilities include a driving range, lessons, club rentals, restaurant, lounge, and golf shop. Fees, including carts, are about $42 in winter, $25 off-season.

If you have reciprocal privileges, **University Park Country Club,** west of I-75 on University Parkway (☎ **941/359-9999**), is Sarasota's only nationally ranked course.

KAYAKING

Sarasota Bay Explorers (☎ **941/388-4200**), at Mote Marine Aquarium (see "Exploring the Area," below), uses a 38-foot pontoon boat to ferry both novice and experienced kayakers and their craft to a marine sanctuary, where everyone paddles through tunnels formed by mangroves to visit the creatures. The paddling is easy, and the waters are shallow. Experienced naturalists serve as guides. Wear swimsuits and tennis shoes or rubber-soled booties, and bring a towel and lunch. The 3-hour trips cost $50 for adults, $40 for children 5 to 17, free for kids under 5 (seats are provided for the youngsters). Call for reservations.

Kayak Treks, 3667 Bahia Vista St. on the mainland (☎ **941/ 365-3892;** fax 941/365-3892; www.kayaktreks.com), has escorted kayak adventures on the area's backwaters, at $35 to $40 per person for half-day trips, $50 to $70 for full-day voyages, and $40 to $50 per person for moonlight cruises on Sarasota Bay. Full-day trips include lunch, and moonlight guests get coffee and dessert. Call for schedule and reservations. The company also rents kayaks.

SAILING

The 41-foot, 12-passenger sailboat *Enterprise,* docked at Marina Jack's Marina, U.S. 41 at Island Park Circle (☎ **941/951-1833**), cruises the waters of both Sarasota Bay and the Gulf of Mexico. Half-day cruises cost $35; the sunset cruise, $20. Departure times vary, and reservations are required.

Siesta Key Sailing, 1219 Southport Dr. (☎ **941/346-7245;** http://hometown.aol.com/treedsail/1.htm; e-mail: treedsail@ aol.com), has half-day, full-day, and 2-day cruises, ranging from $50 to $325 per person, respectively. Reservations are essential.

SPECTATOR SPORTS

Ed Smith Stadium, 2700 12th St., at Tuttle Avenue (☎ **941/ 954-4464**), is the winter home of the **Cincinnati Reds,** who hold spring training here in February and March. East of downtown, the stadium seats 7,500 fans. Admission is $5 to $12. From April to August, the stadium is home to the **Sarasota Red Sox** (☎ **941/365-4460,** ext. 2300; www.sarasox.com), a Class A minor league affiliate of the Boston Red Sox.

The **Sarasota Polo Club,** 8201 Polo Club Lane, Sarasota (☎ **941/359-0000**), midway between Sarasota and Bradenton, is the site of weekly polo matches from November through March, on Sunday afternoons. Call for the schedule of matches and admission fees.

WATER SPORTS

You'll find water-sports activities in front of the major hotels out on the keys (see "Where to Stay," below). **Siesta Sports Rentals,** 6551 Midnight Pass Rd. on Siesta Key (☎ **813/346-1797**), rents kayaks and sailboats, plus beach chairs and umbrellas. You can soar above the bay with **Siesta Parasail,** based at CB's Saltwater Outfitters at the western end of the Stickney Point Bridge (☎ **941/349-4400**).

On the mainland, the downtown center for jet-skiing, sailing, and other water-sports activities is **O'Leary's,** in the Island Park Marina, U.S. 41 and Island Park Circle (☎ **941/953-7505**). It's open daily from 8am to 8pm.

5 Exploring the Area

MUSEUMS & ART GALLERIES

✪ **Ringling Museums.** 5401 Bay Shore Rd. at N. Tamiami Trail (U.S. 41).
☎ **941/359-5700,** or 941/351-1660 for recorded information. www.
ringling.org. E-mail: info@ringling.org. Admission $9 adults, $8 seniors, free for
children 12 and under. Daily 10am–5:30pm. Closed New Year's Day, Thanksgiving, Christmas. From downtown, take U.S. 41 north to University Pkwy. and
follow signs to museum.

The top attraction here, this 60-acre site is where showman John
Ringling collected art and built houses on a grand scale. **The
John and Mable Ringling Museum of Art,** in a pink Italian
Renaissance villa, is filled with more than 500 years of European
and American art, including one of the world's most important
collections of grand 17th–century baroque paintings. The old
master collection also includes five world-renowned tapestry cartoons by Peter Paul Rubens and his studio. The museum also
contains collections of decorative arts and traveling exhibits. Built
in 1925 and modeled after a Venetian palace, the Ringlings' 30-
room winter residence **Ca'd'Zan** (House of John) is filled with
personal mementos. The grounds also include **Circus Galleries,**
a building devoted to circus memorabilia including parade wagons,
calliopes, costumes, and colorful posters; a classical courtyard; a
rose garden; a restaurant; a museum shop; and the historic **Asolo
Theater,** a 19th–century Italian court playhouse (see "Sarasota
After Dark," below).

Sarasota Classic Car Museum. 5500 N. Tamiami Trail (at University Pkwy).
☎ **941/355-6228.** www.sarasotacarmuseum.org. Admission $8.50 adults,
$7.65 seniors, $5.75 children 13–17, $4 children 6–12, free for children under
6. Daily 9am–6pm. Take U.S. 41 north of downtown; museum is 2 blocks west
of the airport.

View more than 80 classic and antique autos, from Rolls-Royces
and Pierce Arrows to the four cars used personally by circus czar
John Ringling. In addition, there are more than 1,200 antique
music boxes, from tiny music boxes to a huge 30-foot Belgian
organ. Check out the Penny Arcade with antique games, and grab
a cone at the ice cream and sandwich shop.

Sarasota Visual Art Center. 707 N. Tamiami Trail (at 6th St.). ☎ **941/
365-2032.** Admission $2. Daily 10am–4pm.

Sarasota is home to more than 40 art galleries and exhibition
spaces, all open to the public year-round. A convenient artistic

starting point is this downtown community art center, next to the Sarasota Convention and Visitors Bureau. It contains three galleries and a small sculpture garden, presenting the area's largest display of art by national and local artists, from paintings and pottery to sculpture, cartoons, jewelry, and enamelware. There are also art demonstrations and special events.

PARKS & GARDENS

✪ **Marie Selby Botanical Gardens.** 811 S Palm Ave. (south of U.S. 41). ☎ **941/366-5731.** Fax 941/366-9807. www.selby.org. Admission $8 adults, $4 children 6–11, free for children 5 and under accompanied by an adult. Daily 10am–5pm. Closed Christmas.

A "must see" for serious plant lovers, this peaceful retreat on the bay just south of downtown is said to be the only botanical garden in the world specializing in the preservation, study, and research of epiphytes; that is, "air plants" such as orchids. It's home to more than 20,000 exotic plants, including more than 6,000 orchids, as well as a bamboo pavilion, butterfly and hummingbird garden, medicinal plant garden, waterfall garden, cactus and succulent garden, fernery, hibiscus garden, palm grove, two tropical food gardens, a native shore-plant community, and Selby's home and the Payne Mansion (both on the National Registry).

✪ **Mote Marine Aquarium.** 1600 Ken Thompson Pkwy. (on City Island). ☎ **800/691-MOTE** or 941/388-4441. Admission $10 adults, $7 children 4–17, free for children 3 and under. Nature cruises $24 adults, $20 children 4–17, free for kids under 4. Combination aquarium-cruise tickets $29 adults, $23 children. Daily 10am–5pm. Nature cruises daily 11am, 1:30pm, and 4pm. From St. Armands Circle, go north toward Longboat Key; turn right just before the Lido-Longboat bridge.

Kids get to touch cool stuff like a stingray (minus the stinger, of course) and watch sharks in the shark tank at this excellent aquarium. Part of the noted Mote Marine Laboratory complex, it focuses on the marine life of the Sarasota area and nearby gulf waters. The kids won't believe all the seahorse babies that come from the dad's pouch (one of Mother Nature's strange-but-true surprises). They can see manatees in the Marine Mammal Center, a block's walk from the aquarium. There are also many research-in-progress exhibits. Start by watching the aquarium's 12-minute film on the feeding habits of sharks, then allow at least 90 minutes to take in everything on land and another 90 minutes to take a narrated sea life encounter cruise with **Sarasota Bay Explorers**

(☎ **727/388-4200**). These fun and informative cruises visit a deserted island, and the guides throw out with nets and bring up sea life for inspection. This company has unusual kayaking adventures, too (see "Outdoor Pursuits & Spectator Sports," above).

Pelican Man's Bird Sanctuary. 1708 Ken Thompson Pkwy. ☎ **941/388-4444.** Admission $3 adults, $1 children. Daily 10am–5pm.

Next to the Mote Marine Aquarium (see above), this sanctuary and rehabilitation center treats more than 5,000 injured birds and other wildlife each year. It is home to about 30 species of birds. There's a gift shop with many bird-oriented items for sale.

Sarasota Jungle Gardens. 37–01 Bayshore Rd. ☎ **941/355-5305.** Admission $9 adults, $8 seniors, $5 children 4–12, free for children 3 and under. Daily 9am–5pm. Reptile shows 10am, 2 and 4pm. Bird shows 10:30am, 2:30, and 4:30pm. Closed Christmas. From downtown, take U.S. 41 north to Myrtle Street, turn left, and go 2 blocks.

If you don't mind black Asian leopards, squirrel monkeys, and other animals going stir-crazy in cages, you and the kids should enjoy this commercial park's lush tropical vegetation, cool jungle trails, tropical plants, exotic waterfowl including a resident flock of pink flamingoes, and alligators and other reptiles. The latter includes "Roscoe," a huge Aldabra tortoise similar to those found in the Galapagos Islands. Children like the petting zoo, pony rides, and bird and reptile shows, too.

A NEARBY STATE PARK & THE LIPPIZZAN STALLIONS

About 20 miles southeast of Sarasota, the **Myakka River State Park,** on Fla. 72 about 9 miles east of I-75, is one of Florida's largest, covering more than 35,000 acres of wetlands, prairies, and dense woodlands along the Myakka River. It's an outstanding wildlife sanctuary and breeding ground, home to hundreds of species of plants and animals, including alligators. The park is open daily from 8am to sunset. Admission is $4 per car with two to eight occupants, $2 for car with driver, or $1 per pedestrian or bicyclist. For more information, contact the headquarters at 13207 S.R. 72, Sarasota, FL 34241 (☎ **941/361-6511;** www.dep.state.fl.us/parks/District_4/MyakkaRiver).

The best and certainly easiest way to see the park is on a 1-hour-long nature excursion by boat and tram with **Myakka Wildlife & Nature Tours** (☎ **941/365-0100**). These informative excursions cost $7 for adults, $4 for children 6 to 12, free for kids 5 and under. Call for the schedules, which change seasonally.

Nearby, horse lovers are drawn to the famous **Lippizzan Stallions,** who do their spectacular leaps at the Ottomar Herrmann training grounds, 32755 Singletary Rd., Myakka City (☎ **941/322-1501**), on Thursday, Friday, and Saturday from late December through March (they tour the country the rest of the year). Call for schedule and directions. Admission is by donation.

6 Shopping

Visitors come from all over the world to shop at ✪ **St. Armands Circle,** on St. Armands Key just inside Lido Key. Wander around this outdoor circle of more than 150 international boutiques, gift shops, galleries, restaurants, and nightspots, all surrounded by lush landscaping, patios, and antiques. Pick up a map at the Sarasota Convention and Visitors Bureau (see "Visitor Information," above). Many shops here are comparable to those in Palm Beach and on Naples' Third Avenue South, so check your credit card limits—or resort to some great window shopping. I love to browse through **Global Navigator** (☎ **813/388-4515**), a travel equipment and apparel shop that reminds me of Banana Republic when it carried really cool stuff (open daily 10am to 10pm).

Parking on or near St. Armands Circle can be scarce, and on-street parking is limited to 3 hours. Your best bets are the free, unrestricted lots on Adams Drive at Monroe and Madison drives.

Downtown, the **Burns Court** and **Herald Square** historic districts, centered on Pineapple Avenue south of Ringling Boulevard, have a trove of upscale boutiques and art galleries worth exploring. You can pick from the freshest of Florida's fruits and vegetables at the downtown **farmer's market,** from 7am to noon on Saturday on Lemon Avenue between Main and 1st streets.

Sarasota Square Mall, 8201 S. Tamiami Trail, at Beneva Road (☎ **941/922-9600**), south of downtown, is the area's largest enclosed mall. **Sarasota Outlet Mall,** on University Parkway just west of I-75 (☎ **941/359-2050**), has about 40 of the better-known factory stores.

7 Where to Stay

In addition to the chain hotels listed below, you'll find the **Comfort Inn** (☎ **800/228-5150** or 941/355-7091), **Days Inn Airport** (☎ **800/329-7466** or 941/355-9271), and **Hampton Inn** (☎ **800/336-9335** or 941/351-7734) standing side by side on Tamiami Trail (U.S. 41) just south of the airport and near the Ringling Museums and the Asolo Center for the Performing Arts. All are of recent vintage and thoroughly modern. A **Courtyard by Marriott** (☎ **800/321-2211** or 941/355-3337) and a **Sleep Inn** (☎ **800/627-5447** or 941/359-8558) are nearby on University Parkway opposite the airport. The **Wellesley Inn & Suites,** 1803 N. Tamiami Trail (U.S. 41, at 18th St.; ☎ **800/444-8888** or 941/366-5128), is the closest chain motel to downtown.

With the beaches here virtually lined with condominiums, it's not surprising that the Resort at Longboat Key Club and the Colony Beach & Tennis Resort (see below) actually are all condo projects operated as hotels. The annual visitors guide published by the Sarasota Convention and Visitors Bureau (see "Visitors Information," above) is a good starting point for finding other options. Among the rental agencies requiring stays of less than a month are **Argus Property Management,** 1200 Siesta Bayside, Sarasota, FL 34242 (☎ **800/237-2252** or 941/346-3499; fax 941/349-6156; www.argusmgmt.com); **Longboat Accommodations,** 4030 Gulf of Mexico Dr., Longboat Key, FL 34228 (☎ **800/237-9505** or 941/383-9505; fax 941/383-1830; www.longboatkey.com); and **Michael Saunders & Company,** 100 S. Washington Blvd., Sarasota, FL 34236 (☎ **800/ 881-2222** or 941/951-6668; www.michaelsaunders.com).

The hotels below are organized by geographic region: on the mainland, on Lido Key, on Longboat Key, and on Siesta Key. Some of the Longboat Key hotels mentioned below actually are in Manatee County, about halfway between Bradenton and downtown Sarasota.

The high season here is from January to April. Rates are usually higher along the beaches at all times, so bargain hunters should stick to the downtown area and commute to the beach. The hotel tax here is 9%.

ON THE MAINLAND

Best Western Midtown. 1425 S. Tamiami Trail (U.S. 41, at Prospect St.), Sarasota, FL 34239. ☎ **800/722-8227,** 800/528-1234, or 941/955-9841. Fax 941/954-8948. www.bwmidtown.com. E-mail: bestwestern@earthlink.net. 100 units. A/C TV TEL. Winter $99–$119 double. Off-season $69–$89 double. Rates include continental breakfast. AE, DC, DISC, MC, V.

Location is the buzzword here, as this L-shaped two- and three-story hotel is 2 miles in either direction from the main causeways leading to the keys. Although positioned next to the Midtown

Plaza shopping center, it's set back from the busy U.S. 41. Tropical palms and plantings surround a heated outdoor swimming pool and sundeck. Guests can graze a buffet-style breakfast, and there's a coin laundry. The rooms are modern and cheery, with light woods and Florida pastel tones. Some of them have kitchenettes.

Hyatt Sarasota. 1000 Blvd. of the Arts, Sarasota, FL 34236. ☎ **800/ 233-1234** or 941/953-1234. Fax 941/952-1987. 297 units. A/C TV TEL. Winter $195–$225 double. Off-season $145–$159 double. AE, DC, DISC, MC, V.

Located beside Sarasota Bay and boasting its own marina, this 10-story tower is the downtown area's centerpiece hotel. Attracting business travelers and groups, it sits adjacent to the Civic Center, the Van Wezel Performing Arts Hall, and the Sarasota Garden Club and is within walking distance of downtown shops and restaurants. The contemporary bedrooms have balconies overlooking the marina or bay; they have coffeemakers, hair dryers, and irons and boards.

Dining/Diversions: The main dining room, Scalini, features Mediterranean cuisine. Out on the docks, the publike Boathouse offers casual fare and water views of the marina. Inside, Tropics Lounge provides libations.

Amenities: Concierge, room service, valet parking and laundry, newspaper delivery, business center, airport shuttle ($3 per person), heated outdoor swimming pool, patio, health club, marina.

Southland Inn Motel. 2229 N. Tamiami Trail (U.S. 41), Sarasota, FL 34234. ☎ **941/954-5775.** Fax 941/364-8329. E-mail: devdante@prodigy.net. 31 units. A/C TV TEL. Winter $45–$95 single or double. Off-season $25–$55 single or double. Weekly rates available. MC, V.

One of several older mom-and-pop motels on busy U.S. 41, a few minutes north of downtown, this two-story complex has an outdoor pool and a guest laundry. More than half the units are efficiencies or apartments with kitchens, but they usually are rented on a weekly basis during winter.

LIDO KEY
✪ **Half Moon Beach Club.** 2050 Ben Franklin Dr. (at Taft Dr.), Sarasota, FL 34236. ☎ **800/358-3245** or 941/388-3694. Fax 941/388-1938. www. halfmoon-lidokey.com. E-mail: info@halfmoon-lidokey.com. 85 units. A/C MINI-BAR TV TEL. Winter $129–$229 double. Off-season $89–$189 double. AE, DC, DISC, MC, V.

Near the south end of Lido, this two-story art deco–style hotel is right on the beach and less than half a block from South Lido Beach Park. The front of the building forms a circle around a small but very attractive courtyard with a heated pool and sunning area. From there, guests take a hallway through a motel-style block of rooms to the beach, where they can rent cabanas and order libation to be delivered from the bar inside. The spacious guest rooms are furnished with light woods and have refrigerators. Some also have kitchenettes with microwave ovens, but only the four beachfront rooms have gulf views. Facilities include Seagrapes, an indoor/outdoor restaurant; an outdoor heated swimming pool; volleyball; a gulf-front sundeck; a coin laundry; and bike and video rentals. Complimentary newspapers are delivered to the rooms each morning.

Holiday Inn Lido Beach. 233 Ben Franklin Dr. (at Thoreau Dr.), Sarasota, FL 34236. ☎ **800/892-9174** or 941/388-5555. Fax 941/388-4321. 135 units. A/C TV TEL. Winter $179–$319 double. Off-season $125–$235 double. AE, DC, MC, V.

Conveniently located at the north end of Lido, this modern seven-story hotel is within walking distance of St. Armands Circle. Unfortunately, the beach across the street isn't the best stretch of sand here. The bedrooms have balconies that face the gulf or the bay and are furnished with light woods and pastel fabrics. The rooftop restaurant and lounge offers panoramic views of the Gulf of Mexico. There're also a lobby lounge and a casual pool bar. Amenities include valet laundry, coin laundry, newspaper delivery, outdoor heated swimming pool with gulf view, bicycle rentals, water-sports equipment.

LONGBOAT KEY

✪ **Colony Beach & Tennis Resort.** 1620 Gulf of Mexico Dr., Longboat Key, FL 34228. ☎ **800/4-COLONY** or 941/383-6464. Fax 941/383-7549. www.colonybeachresort.com. E-mail: colonyfl@ix.netcom.com. 235 units. A/C TV TEL. Winter $300–$450 suite. Off-season $190–$350 suite. Packages available. AE, DISC, MC, V.

Sitting 3 miles north of St. Armands Circle, this beachside facility is consistently rated one of the nation's finest tennis resorts. The beachside Colony Restaurant and swimming pool date from 1952 when this was a beach club, but today's accommodations are in modern, luxurious one- and two-bedroom condo apartments—complete with living rooms, dining areas, fully equipped kitchenettes, and sun balconies—and three private cottages right on the superb beach (they are most expensive units here). They are built around 21 tennis courts, two of them lighted for night play. A staff of professionals conducts highly acclaimed programs for adults and children.

Dining/Diversions: One of the finest dining venues here, the beachside Colony Restaurant offers continental cuisine for lunch and dinner (jackets requested for men at dinner). Sharing the old building, the informal dining room provides breakfast, lunch, and dinner. The poolside Colony Patio & Bar has casual dining. The lavish Sunday brunch here is popular with locals as well as out-of-towners. The Colony Lounge has nightly entertainment.

Amenities: Concierge, laundry and dry cleaning, child care, valet parking, courtesy limo, outstanding year-round supervised children's programs for ages 3 to 12, health spa, complimentary tennis, beachfront swimming pool, fitness center, golf, deep-sea fishing, water sports, aerobic classes, bicycle rental, boutiques, beauty salon.

Holiday Inn Hotel & Suites. 4949 Gulf of Mexico Dr., Longboat Key, FL 34228. ☎ **800/HOLIDAY** or 941/383-3771. Fax 941/383-7871. www. hilongboat.com. E-mail: holidaylongboat@mindspring.com. 146 units. A/C TV TEL. Winter $189–$259 double; $229–$329 suite. Off-season $129–$229 double; $159–$299 suite. AE, DC, DISC, MC, V.

In Manatee County about halfway up Longboat Key, 8 miles north of St. Armands Circle, this family-oriented beachside motel is built around an indoor courtyard with a swimming pool, whirlpool, games area, and Longboat Key's only fast-food outlets (Pizza Hut, Nathan's Famous, Mrs. Field's Cookies, and Seattle's Best Coffee). The enclosed area makes this a good respite on rainy days or during a cool snap. The contemporary rooms and suites have patios or balconies, with the choice units facing the beach. All units have coffeemakers and refrigerators.

Dining: In addition to the fast-food outlets, there's a restaurant with adjacent clubby bar plus a beachside snack bar.

Amenities: Concierge, limited room service, laundry and dry cleaning, indoor and outdoor pools and whirlpools, four lighted tennis courts, exercise room with sauna, gift shops, guest laundry, bicycle rental, water sports.

✪ **Longboat Key Hilton Beach Resort.** 4711 Gulf of Mexico Dr., Longboat Key, FL 34228. ☎ **800/282-3046** or 941/383-2451. Fax 941/383-7979. 102 units. A/C MINIBAR TV TEL. Winter $195–$295 double; $275–$375 suite. Off-season $140–$200 double; $225–$315 suite. Packages available. AE, DC, MC, V.

Also in Manatee County, 7$^{1}/_{2}$ miles north of St. Armands Circle, this five-story concrete building is surrounded by lush foliage and gardens. A much more charming gray wooden structure to one side holds all of the public facilities and more than makes up for the blandness of the rooms' building. The bar and pool area here are pleasant areas for relaxing lunches or sunset cocktails. Recently refurbished, the bedrooms are furnished in a tropical style. Most have a patio or narrow balcony. A few gulf-front rooms are the most expensive.

Dining: The main restaurant offers great views of the gulf to accompany a seafood menu, while the poolside bar serves lunch and beverages.

Amenities: Room service, valet laundry, free shuttle to St. Armands Key for shopping, heated outdoor swimming pool, private beach, bicycle and water-sports equipment rentals, one tennis court, shuffleboard.

✪ **The Resort at Longboat Key Club.** 301 Gulf of Mexico Dr. (P.O. Box 15000), Longboat Key, FL 34228. ☎ **800/237-8821** or 941/383-8821. Fax 941/383-0359. www.longboatkeyclub.com. 232 units. A/C TV TEL. Winter $200–$985 suite. Off-season $140–$500 suite. Packages available off-season. AE, DISC, MC, V. From St. Armands Key, take Gulf of Mexico Drive north, take first left after bridge.

Part of a real estate development on 410 acres at the southern end of Longboat Key, this award-winning condo resort pampers the country-club set with upscale restaurants and a variety of recreational activities in a lush tropical setting. The spacious and luxurious suites have private balconies overlooking the Gulf of Mexico, a lagoon, or golf course fairways. All have custom-designed furnishings and neo-classical decor. All but 20 units have full kitchens.

Dining/Diversions: Orchid's Restaurant has the feel of an informal but elegant supper club, serving classical Italian cuisine in a romantic setting, while the adjacent Orchid's Lounge offers casual dining and live entertainment. Barefoots Bar & Grille offers relaxed poolside dining. Overlooking the Islandside Golf Course, Spike 'n Tees serves breakfast and lunch in an outdoor setting. At Harborside Marina, the dining room offers nightly theme buffets, while breakfast, lunch, and dinner are served at The Grille.

Amenities: Concierge, room service (7am to midnight), valet laundry, child care, supervised children's activities (in summer), in-room massage, newspaper delivery. Two golf courses (45 holes), golf school, two tennis centers (38 courts), 500 feet of beach with water sports, exercise track, steam rooms, jogging paths, nature trails, swimming pool, whirlpool, bicycle rentals, tour desk, boutiques.

SIESTA KEY

Best Western Siesta Beach Resort. 5311 Ocean Blvd. (at Calle Miramar), Sarasota, FL 34242. ☎ **800/223-5786** or 941/349-3211. Fax 941/349-7915. 53 units. A/C TV TEL. Winter $149–$158 double; $189–$275 suite. Off-season $84–$89 double; $104–$165 suite. Weekly rates available. AE, DC, DISC, MC, V.

In Siesta Village on the northern end of the key, this older but well maintained motel has two buildings across a side street from each other. It offers standard hotel rooms and one- and two-bedroom suites, all decorated in pastel tones with light woods. The suites have kitchenettes. Facilities include a heated swimming pool, whirlpool, and guest laundry. There's no restaurant on the premises, but the Blase Cafe and other outlets are across the street. Public beach access also is across the street, and Siesta Key Public Beach is about ¹/₂ mile away.

☻ **Captiva Beach Resort.** 6772 Sara Sea Circle, Siesta Key, FL 34242. ☎ **800/349-4131** or 941/349-4131. Fax 941/349-8141. www. captivabeachresort.com. E-mail: info@captivabeachresort.com. 20 units. A/C TV TEL. Winter $120–$290. Off-season $75–$180. Weekly and monthly rates available. AE, DISC, MC, V.

Owners Robert and Jane Ispaso have substantially upgraded and improved this older property about half a block from the beach on a narrow, closely packed circle populated by other small motels. Every one of the comfortable, sparkling-clean units here has some form of cooking facilities, and some have separate living rooms with sleeper sofas. These are older buildings, so you'll find window air conditioners mounted through the walls, and shower-only bathrooms in some units. It's very popular with longer term guests during winter, so you'll get fresh towels daily but maid service only once a week (there is a coin laundry here). This and the circle's other motels share a common pool area. There's no restaurant on the premises, but there are several just a short walk away in the Stickney Point commercial area.

☻ **Turtle Beach Resort.** 9049 Midnight Pass Rd., Sarasota, FL 34242. ☎ **941/349-4554.** Fax 941/312-9034. www.turtlebeachresort.com. E-mail: turtlebch1@aol.com. 10 units. A/C TV TEL. Winter $1,275–$1,975 per week double. Off-season $140–$235 per day double. AE, DISC, MC, V. Pets accepted at extra charge.

On Siesta Key's south end near Turtle Beach, this intimate little bay-side charmer began life years ago as a traditional Old Florida fishing camp. In the early 1990s, owners Gail and Dave

Rubinfeld renovated the five original clapboard cottages (still the preferable choice for charm), and added five units in a rustic but modern motel-style building (these are larger but lack great water views). The complex is tightly packed, and although some units are very close to a small bayside swimming pool, heavy tropical foliage provides a reasonable degree of privacy, and high wooden fences surround each unit's private whirlpool.

The cottages are done in Victorian, Southwest, Key West, Caribbean, country French, and traditional American country decor. The living room of the American country model sits, docklike, right on the bay (it's justifiably the honeymoon cottage), and the Southwest model looks across the bayside pool to the water. There's no restaurant on the grounds, but Ophelia's on the Bay seafood restaurant next door was once the old fishing camp's dining room, and two units have kitchens (all have microwave ovens and coffeemakers). Guests can use fishing poles and paddleboats. No smoking is allowed inside. Winter rentals are by the week, but you might be able to get a few nights if there's a vacancy.

8 Where to Dine

The restaurants below are organized geographically: on the mainland, on St. Armands Key (next to Lido Key), and on Siesta Key.

ON THE MAINLAND

You'll find most of the national chain fast-food and family restaurants along U.S. 41.

MODERATE

✪ **Bijou Cafe.** 1287 1st St. (at Pineapple Ave.). ☎ **941/366-8111.** Reservations recommended. Main courses $16–$24. AE, DC, MC, V. Mon–Thurs 11:30am–2pm and 5–9:30pm, Fri 11:30am–2pm and 5–10:30pm, Sat 5–10:30pm, Sun 5–9:30pm. Closed Sun June–Dec. Free valet parking nightly in winter, weekends off-season. INTERNATIONAL.

Locals always recommend the award-winning cuisine at chef Jean-Pierre Knaggs' charming cafe in the heart of the theater district. He masterfully prepares and artfully presents the likes of prime veal Louisville (with crushed pecans and bourbon-pear sauce), pan-seared crab cakes served under a remoulade and over a bed of fresh green, and gently simmered lamb shanks with rosemary and garlic. The outstanding wine list has won accolades from *Wine Spectator* magazine.

Cafe of the Arts. 5230 N. Tamiami Trail (south of University Pkwy.).
☎ **941/351-4304.** Reservations recommended. Main courses $12–$28.
AE, DISC, MC, V. Mon–Fri 11am–3pm and 5–9pm, Sat–Sun 9am–3pm and
5–9pm. Closed June–Sept. FRENCH.

Warm and soothing hospitality with a French flair welcomes you
to Alain Taulere's café-bakery-wine bar, in a Spanish-style building across from the Ringling museum complex. He offers an artsy
ambience in several dining rooms, one of which spans the rear of
the building and enjoys a view out to a lush tropical courtyard.
It's a much bigger establishment than at first meets the eye, but
volume results in reasonable prices for this quality French fare.
Dinner dishes range from heart-healthy vegetable platters to rack
of lamb dijonnais. Don't leave until you sample the chocolate
eclair or strawberry mousse. The popular Saturday and Sunday
brunch features both breakfast and lunch selections.

Marina Jack. In Island Park, Bayfront at Central Ave. ☎ **941/365-4232.**
Reservations recommended in dining room, not accepted in lounge and raw
bar. Dining room main courses $15–$27. Lounge and raw bar sandwiches and
salads $6–$9, main courses $9–$20. AE, MC, V. Dining room daily noon–3pm
and 5–10pm. Lounge and raw bar Mon–Sat 11:45am–3pm and 5–10pm, Sun
noon–10pm. SEAFOOD/CONTINENTAL.

Overlooking the waterfront with a wraparound 270° view of
Sarasota Bay and Siesta and Lido keys, this two-restaurants-in-
one establishment has spectacular water vistas and a carefree "on
vacation" attitude, especially on the open-air raw bar deck, which
usually is packed all afternoon on weekends and at sunset every
day. You'll have to wait for a table or barstool down here, but be
sure to make reservations if you attempt to have a meal in the
upstairs dining room. The menu in both venues offers fresh
native seafood, with grilled grouper your best bet upstairs and as
a sandwich downstairs. The downstairs lounge and raw bar add
other sandwiches and burgers. The food is good but not the best
in town, so come here for a relaxing, fun time.

✪ **Michael's on East.** 1212 East Ave. S. (between Bahia and Prospect sts.).
☎ **941/366-0007.** Reservations recommended. Main courses $16.50–$32.
AE, DC, MC, V. Winter Mon–Fri 11:30am–2pm, daily 5:30–10pm. Off-season
Mon–Fri 11:30am–2pm, Mon–Sat 6–10pm. Complimentary valet parking.
CREATIVE INTERNATIONAL.

At the rear of the Midtown Plaza shopping center on U.S. 41
south of downtown, Michael Klauber's chic bistro is one of the top
places here for fine dining, and the local's favorite after-theater

haunt. Huge cut-glass walls create three intimate dining areas, one with a black marble bar for pre- or after-dinner drinks. Prepared with fresh ingredients and a creative flair, the offerings here will tempt your taste buds. The menu changes with the seasons. In autumn, you might start with yellowfin tuna sashimi with a vegetable sushi roll and caviar. From there, you could progress to slightly spicy Louisiana-style crab cakes, seared Chilean sea bass with couscous and artichoke hearts in a thyme-accented tomato coulis, or perhaps grilled duck breast with Napa cabbage, sweet potato, and smoked bacon in an apple cider reduction. A light fare menu goes until midnight, and there's dancing in the lounge starting at 9:30pm.

INEXPENSIVE

First Watch. 1395 Main St. (at Central and Pineapple aves.). ☎ **941/ 954-1395.** Reservations not accepted. Breakfast $3–$6.50; sandwiches and salads, $5–$6.50. AE, DISC, MC, V. Daily 7:30am–2:30pm. AMERICAN.

This bright dining room with natural wood Windsor chairs at oak-trimmed tables is the downtown place for breakfast or lunch (it's usually packed on weekend mornings, so be prepared to wait). Traditional breakfast offerings range widely, from bacon and eggs and omelettes to a skillet layered with eggs and vegetables. There are several healthy choices, too, such as oatmeal cooked with cinnamon and apples. Lunch adds sandwiches on fresh bread and creative salads, including a tasty white-meat chicken version with raisins and crunchy water chestnuts.

If the wait's too long, walk south along Main Street to Palm Avenue. This block has several coffeehouses and cafes with sidewalk seating.

Patrick's. 1400 Main St. (at Pineapple and Central aves.). ☎ **941/ 952-1170.** Reservations not accepted. Sandwiches and burgers $5.50–$7; main courses $11–$15. AE, MC, V. Daily 11am–midnight (Sun brunch 11am–3pm). AMERICAN.

With a semicircular facade, this informal, polished-oak and brass-rail brasserie offers wide-windowed views of downtown's main intersection. The decor also boasts hanging plants and ceiling fans, plus a unique collection of sports memorabilia. The menu offers a range of pub fare: steaks and chops, burgers, seafood, pastas, pizzas, salads, sandwiches, and omelettes; plus veal piccata, française, or marsala; broiled salmon with dill-hollandaise sauce; and sesame chicken.

⭘ **Yoder's.** 3434 Bahia Vista St. (west of Beneva Rd.). ☎ **941/955-7771.** Reservations not accepted. Breakfast $2–$6; sandwiches and burgers $3–$6; main courses $5–$12. No credit cards. Mon–Sat 6am–8pm. AMISH/ AMERICAN.

It's worth driving about 3 miles east of downtown to check out this good-value, award-winning eatery operated by an Amish family (both Sarasota and Bradenton have sizable Amish communities). Evoking the Pennsylvania Dutch country, the simple dining room displays handcrafts, photos, and paintings celebrating the Amish way. The menu emphasizes plain, made-from-scratch cooking such as home-style meat loaf, baked and southern fried chicken, country-smoked ham, and fried fillet of flounder. Burgers, salads, soups, and sandwiches are also available. Leave room for Mrs. Yoder's traditional shoo-fly and other homemade pies, one of the biggest draws here. There's neither alcohol nor smoking here. They don't take credit cards, but there's an ATM near the entrance.

ST. ARMANDS KEY

Plan to spend at least one evening at St. Armands Circle. The nighttime scene here is like a fair, with locals and visitors alike strolling around the circle, poking their heads into a few stores, which stay open after dark and window-shopping the others. It's fun and safe, so come early and plan to stay late. See "Shopping," above, for parking tips.

Instead of ordering dessert after your meal, wander on over to **Kilwin's,** 312 John Ringling Blvd. (☎ **941/388-3200**), for some gourmet chocolate, Mackinac Island fudge, or ice cream or yogurt in a homemade waffle cone. It's open Sunday to Thursday until 10:30pm, Friday and Saturday until 11pm.

EXPENSIVE

Cafe l'Europe. 431 St. Armands Circle (at John Ringling Blvd.). ☎ **941/388-4415.** Reservations recommended. Main courses $17–$26. AE, DC, DISC, MC, V. Daily 11am–4pm and 5–10pm. CONTINENTAL.

As its name implies, a European atmosphere prevails at this consistently excellent restaurant, with a decor of brick walls and arches, dark woods, brass fixtures, pink linens, and hanging plants. The menu offers selections ranging from a Tuscan-style mixture of seafood in a rich broth over fusilli pasta to a veal tenderloin glazed with balsamic vinegar and served with a rich blackberry and port wine sauce.

MODERATE

Charley's Crab. 420 St. Armands Circle (between John Ringling Blvd. and Blvd. of the Presidents). ☎ **941/388-3964.** Reservations recommended. Main courses $15–$25; dinner sandwiches $9–$11. AE, DC, MC, V. Mon–Sat 11:30am–4pm and 5–10:30pm, Sun noon–4pm and 5–10pm. SEAFOOD.

A favorite for people watching, Charley's is popular not just for crab cakes and crab fettuccine (with mushrooms, tomatoes, and basil in a herbed shrimp sauce), but for a full range of fresh seafood dishes (if the local fishers haven't caught any fish today, it's flown in via FedEx). Up to 10 varieties of excellent wine are available by the glass. Alfresco diners fill sidewalk tables early at lunch and dinner as shoppers stroll past. A pianist adds to the lively outdoor atmosphere. Large windows in the comfortable indoor dining room give a great view of the passing parade as well.

✪ **Hemingway's.** 325 John Ringling Blvd. ($^1/_2$ block off St. Armands Circle). ☎ **941/388-3948.** Reservations recommended. Main courses $12–$22; dinner sandwiches $8–$11. AE, DC, DISC, MC, V. Sun–Thurs 11:30am–10pm, Fri–Sat 11:30am–11pm. FLORIDIAN/CARIBBEAN.

For a casual spot with an eclectic "Floribbean" menu and a large bar with a friendly, laid-back Key West ambience, take the elevator or climb the winding stairs to this above-the-mob second-floor hideaway. Hemingway's is charming and comfortable in the best Old Florida tradition. The decor features a mix of green floral booths and tables with rattan chairs. You might start with gator bits or conch fritters, then choose from an evenly distributed mix of seafood, barbecued ribs, and other meats. Mariner's shrimp is a healthy winner: They're perfectly charcoal grilled, basted with a light teriyaki sauce, and served over rice with fresh asparagus and baby carrots.

INEXPENSIVE

Blue Dolphin Cafe. 470 John Ringling Blvd. (1 block off St. Armand's Circle). ☎ **941/388-3566.** Reservations not accepted. Breakfast $4.50–$7; sandwiches, burgers, salads $5–$7. No credit cards. Daily 7am–3pm. AMERICAN/DINER.

On the John Ringling Boulevard spoke of St. Armands Circle, this plain, informal diner is this affluent area's only inexpensive place to have breakfast or lunch. It offers standard breakfast fare (as well as a wrap of scrambled eggs, chili, and cheddar cheese topped with sour cream and green onions) and lunch choices plus chicken fajita sandwiches, homemade chili, and a wrap enclosing Thai-style stir-fried vegetables. You can order breakfast anytime.

SIESTA KEY

Ocean Boulevard, which runs through **Siesta Village,** the area's funky, laid-back beach hangout, is virtually lined with restaurants and pubs, including Blase Cafe (see below). Most have outdoor seating and bars, which attract the beach crowd during the day. At night rock-and-roll bands draw teenagers and college students to this lively scene.

✪ **Blase Cafe.** In Village Corner, 5263 Ocean Blvd. (at Calle Miramar), Siesta Village. ☎ **941/349-9822.** Reservations not accepted. Breakfast $5–$8; lunch $5–$9; main courses $9–$17. No credit cards. Daily 9am–9:30pm. Closed Mon June–Nov. INTERNATIONAL.

One of Florida's most unusual restaurants, this super-casual, al fresco establishment has a few tables under cover of the Village Corner shopping center's walkway, but most guests sit at umbrella tables on a wooden deck built around a palm tree in the center's asphalt parking lot. Never mind the cars pulling in and out virtually next to your chair: The food here is so good and inexpensive that it draws droves of locals, who don't mind waiting for a table (a Chinese carryout shares the deck, so reservations are impossible). This is the key's best breakfast spot, offering Italian- and Louisiana-flavored fritattas as well as plain old bacon-and-eggs. Lunch sees big salads and platters such as chicken Alfredo and Florentine crepes with shrimp. At night, chefs who've previously worked at St. Armands Circle's upscale restaurants come on duty and put forth the likes of shrimp Vera Cruz—sauteed with tomatoes, mushrooms, and artichoke hearts in a delightfully light basil cream sauce.

Turtles. 8875 Midnight Pass Rd. (at Turtle Beach Rd.). ☎ **941/346-2207.** Reservations not accepted. Salads and sandwiches $6–$9; main courses $10–$16; early bird specials $9. AE, DC, DISC, MC, V. Winter daily 11:30am–10pm. Off-season daily 11:30am–9:30pm. Early bird specials daily 4–6pm. AMERICAN.

With tropical overtones and breathtaking water vistas across from Turtle Beach, this informal restaurant on Little Sarasota Bay has tables both indoors and on an outside deck at which to try dishes such as snapper New Orleans, Florida-style blue crab cakes, or steak under a Jack Daniels whiskey sauce. There's a selection of pastas and platters to devour. The early bird specials include a medium-sized fish portion.

9   Sarasota After Dark

The cultural capital of Florida's west coast, Sarasota is home to a host of performing arts, especially during the winter season. To get the latest update on what's happening any time of year, call the city's 24-hour **Artsline** (☎ **941/365-ARTS**). Also check the "Ticket" section in Friday's *Herald-Tribune,* the local daily newspaper; the Sarasota Convention and Visitors Bureau usually has copies (see "Essentials," above).

THE PERFORMING ARTS

The official State Theater of Florida since 1965, the ✪ **FSU Center for the Performing Arts (Asolo Theatre),** at the Ringling Museums, 5555 N. Tamiami Trail (U.S. 41), (☎ **941/ 351-8000;** www.asolo.org), presents the winter-through-spring Asolo Theatre Festival, a program of ballet and Broadway-style musicals and drama. The main stage, the 487-seat Harold E. and Ethel M. Mertz Theatre, is an attraction in itself—the former Dumfermline Opera House, originally constructed in Scotland in 1900 and transferred piece by piece to Sarasota in 1987. The 161-seat Asolo Conservatory Theatre was later added as a smaller venue for experimental and alternative offerings.

Free guided tours of the center are offered Wednesday to Saturday from 10 to 11:30am, except from June to August and during technical rehearsals between plays; call for tour times.

Downtown, the lavender, seashell-shaped **Van Wezel Performing Arts Hall,** 777 N. Tamiami Trail (U.S. 41), at 9th Street (☎ **800/826-9303** or 941/953-3366; www.vanwezel.org), is visible for miles on the bay-front skyline. It offers excellent visual and acoustic conditions, with year-round programs ranging from symphony and jazz concerts, opera, musical comedy, and choral productions to ballet and international productions. It's the home of the Florida West Coast Symphony, the Jazz Club of Sarasota, the Sarasota Pops, the Sarasota Ballet of Florida, and the Sarasota Concert Band.

Downtown Sarasota's theater district is home to the **Florida Studio Theatre,** 1241 N. Palm Ave., at Cocoanut Avenue (☎ **941/366-9796**), which has contemporary performances from December to August, including a New Play Festival in May. Built in 1926 as the Edwards Theater, **The Opera House,** 61 N. Pineapple Ave., between Main and 1st streets (☎ **941/953-7030;**

www.sarasotaopera.org), hosts the Sarasota Opera in February and March, while the Sarasota Ballet and other companies take the stage the rest of the year. Next door to The Opera House, the **Golden Apple Dinner Theatre,** 25 N. Pineapple Ave. (☎ 941/366-5454), presents cocktails, dinner, and a professional Broadway-style show year-round. The professional, nonequity **Theatre Works,** 1247 1st St., at Cocoanut Ave. (☎ 941/952-9170), presents musical revues and other works all year.

THE CLUB & MUSIC SCENE

You can find plenty of music to dance to on the mainland at **Sarasota Quay,** the downtown waterfront dining-shopping-entertainment complex on Tamiami Trail (U.S. 41) a block north of John Ringling Causeway. Just walk around this brick building and your ears will take you to the action. The laser sound-and-light crowd gathers at **In Extremis** (☎ 941/954-2008), where a high-energy deejay spins Top 40 tunes. **Downunder Jazz Bar** (☎ 941/951-2467) offers contemporary jazz. Michael's Seafood Grill turns into **Anthony's After Dark** rocking disco at 10:30pm.

And don't forget the evening entertainment at **Marina Jack** and **Michael's on East** (see "Where to Dine," above).

Over on St. Armands Circle, the Patio Lounge in Columbia restaurant (☎ 941/388-3987) is one of the liveliest spots along the beach strip, featuring live, high-energy dance music on Tuesday to Sunday evenings. And on Siesta Key, the pubs and restaurants along Ocean Boulevard in Siesta Village have noisy rock-and-roll bands entertaining a mostly young crowd (see "Where to Dine," above).

6

Bradenton &
Anna Maria Island

*V*isitors often overlook Bradenton as they speed south on their way to Sarasota and beyond. But here you can visit "Snooty" the famous manatee, and you can take an entire vacation on **Anna Maria Island,** northernmost in the chain of barrier islands stretching from Tampa Bay to Sarasota. Anna Maria claims 7¹/₂ miles of white-sand beaches—but no glitzy resorts, just casual island getaways. The island's communities—Bradenton Beach, Holmes Beach, and Anna Maria—are popular with family vacationers and seniors, offering a variety of public beaches, fishing piers, bungalows, low-rise motels, and a terrific bed-and-breakfast. You can have a very relaxing beach vacation here without the bustle and out-of-sight prices found across the bridge on Sarasota's Longboat Key.

Bradenton and Manatee County also own the northern half of Longboat Key. Most of Longboat's resorts are closer to Sarasota than to Bradenton, so I have included them in chapter 5. On the northern tip of Longboat, the little fishing village of Longbeach was established in 1885 and still has some remnants of Old Florida.

1 Orientation

ARRIVING
Bradenton and Anna Maria Island share **Sarasota-Bradenton International Airport** with Sarasota (see "Orientation," in chapter 5).

VISITOR INFORMATION
For a packet of information about Bradenton, Anna Maria Island, and surrounding Manatee County, contact the **Greater Bradenton Area Convention and Visitors Bureau,** P.O. Box 1000, Bradenton, FL 34206 (☎ **800/4-MANATEE** or 941/729-9177; fax 941/729-1820; www.floridaislandbeaches.org).

For maps, brochures, and information, call or drop by the **Manatee County Tourist Information Center,** on U.S. 301 just west of Exit 43 off I-75 (☎ **941/729-7040**). Open daily except holidays from 8:30am to 5:30pm, it has a volunteer staff on hand to answer your questions and sells excellent road maps for half off the list price. The office has an information kiosk in front of the Vanity Fair store the **Prime Outlets,** across I-75. It's open Monday to Saturday 10am to 6pm, Sunday 11am to 6pm.

The **Anna Maria Island Chamber of Commerce,** 5337 Gulf Dr. N., Holmes Beach, FL 34217(☎ **941/778-1541;** fax 941/778-9679; www.annamariaislandchamber.org; e-mail: amicc@netsrq.com), publishes an annual visitors guide to the island. Its office in the heart of the Holmes Beach business district is open Monday to Friday 9am to 5pm.

2   Getting Around

Manatee County Area Transit, known locally as **Manatee CAT** (☎ **941/749-7116**), operates scheduled public bus service throughout the area.

Taxi companies include **Bruce's Taxi** (☎ **941/755-6070**), **Checker Cab** (☎ **941/751-3181**), and **Yellow Cab** (☎ **941/748-4800**).

3   Hitting the Beach

Anna Maria Island has four public beaches, all with rest rooms, picnic areas, lifeguards, and free parking. The largest and best is **Coquina Beach,** which occupies the southern mile of the island below Bradenton Beach. It has both gulf and bay sides, is sheltered by whispering Australian pines, and has a nature trail and large parking lots. **Cortez Beach** is in Bradenton Beach, just north of Coquina Beach. In the island's center, **Manatee County Public Beach** is at Gulf Drive. **Holmes Beach** is at the west end of Manatee Avenue (Fla. 64). **Anna Maria Bayfront Park** is on Bay Boulevard at the northwest end of the island, fronting both the bay and the Gulf of Mexico.

4   Outdoor Pursuits & Spectator Sports
BIKING & IN-LINE SKATING
The flat terrain makes for good in-line skating and fine if not challenging bike riding. **Island Rental Service,** 3214 East Bay Dr.

(☎ **800/248-8797** or 941/778-1472), next to Shells restaurant in Holmes Beach, will deliver rental bikes, mopeds, baby strollers, and various beach paraphernalia. Plain bikes start at $7 an hour, $25 a day, while mopeds cost $15 an hour or $25 for half day. Open Monday to Saturday 8am to 6pm, Sunday 10am to 4pm. **Native Rentals,** in S&S Plaza, 5340 Marina Dr. in Holmes Beach (☎ **941/778-7757**), rents bikes starting at $3 an hour or $8 per day, in-line skates for $4 an hour or $15 a day. The office is opposite the BP service station in the Holmes Beach business district. Open Monday to Saturday from 7am to 7pm, Sunday from 9am to 5pm. In Anna Maria village on the island's northern end, **Neumann's Island Beach Store,** 427 Pine Ave., at Tarpon Street (☎ **941/778-3316**), rents bikes for the same price. It's open daily 9am to 5pm (closed Sunday from June to October).

BOATING & FISHING

When Florida's ban on net fishing devastated its traditional business, the village of Cortez on the east side of the Cortez Bridge aimed for another catch: tourist dollars. Here you can go deep-sea fishing with the **Cortez Fleet,** 4330 127th St. W. (☎ **941/794-1223**). Party boat deep-sea fishing voyages range from 4 hours to 9 hours, with prices starting at $28 for adults, $25 for seniors, and $14 for children. Call for the schedules, which can change from day to day.

On Anna Maria Island, you can rent boats from **Bradenton Beach Marina,** 402 Church Ave. (☎ **941/778-2288**); **Captain's Marina,** 5501 Marina Dr., Holmes Beach (☎ **941/778-1977**); and **Five O'Clock Marina,** 412 Pine Ave., Anna Maria (☎ **941/778-5577**). On northern Longboat Key, **Cannons Marina,** 6040 Gulf of Mexico Dr. (☎ **941/383-1311**), also rents boats. Several deep-sea fishing charter boats are based at these marinas.

You also can fish from **Anna Maria City Pier,** on the north end of Anna Maria Island, and at the **Bradenton Beach City Pier,** at Cortez Road. Both are free of charge.

CRUISES

Based in Cortez, the *Cortez Lady* (☎ **941/761-9777**), makes sightseeing cruises usually Tuesday, Thursday, and Saturday to **Egmont Key State Park,** on historic Egmont Key 3 miles off the northern end of Anna Maria Island at the mouth of Tampa Bay (see "Cruises" under "Outdoor Activities" in chapter 4 for more information). You can go snorkeling and shelling here, so bring your swimsuit and gear. This cruise costs $20 for adults, $15 seniors, $10 children 14 and under. Call for the schedules and reservations.

You can also get to Egmont Key on a 30-foot sloop-rigged sailboat with **Spice Sailing Charters** (☎ **941/778-3240**), based at the Galati Yacht Basin on Bay Boulevard on northern Anna Maria Island. The company also has sunset cruises. Call for schedule, prices, and reservations, which are required.

That paddlewheeler you see going up and down the bay is the *Seafood Shack Showboat,* operated by the Seafood Shack restaurant, 4110 127th St. W., in Cortez (☎ **800/299-5048** or 941/794-5048). It has afternoon and sunset cruises to Sarasota Bay, Tampa Bay, and as far away as the Sunshine Skyway. Prices range from $13 to $15 for adults, $11 to $13 for seniors, and $4.71 to $5.66 for children 4 to 11. The *Showboat* goes to a different destination each day, so call for the schedule and reservations.

GOLF

The city and county operate several municipal courses where you can play without breaking your budget.

Locals say they prefer the county's 18-hole, par 72 **Buffalo Creek Golf Course,** on the north side of the river at 8100 Erie Road in Palmetto (☎ **941/776-2611**). At well over 7,000 yards, it's the longest in the area, and lots of water and alligators will keep you entertained. Wintertime greens fees are about $35 with cart, $25 without. They drop to about $18 and $16, respectively, during summer.

You'll pay the same at **Manatee County Golf Course,** 5290 66th St. W. (☎ **941/792-6773**), an 18-hole, par-72 course on the southern rim of the city. Both county courses require that tee times be set up at least 2 days in advance.

Also open to the public, the city's **River Run Golf Links,** 1801 27th St. E. (☎ **941/747-6331**), set beside the Braden River, is an 18-hole, par-70 course with lots of water in its layout. Winter fees here are about $26 with cart, $17 walking. They're about $16 riding, $8 walking in summer. A 2-day advance notice is required for tee times here, too.

Other courses include the **Palma Sola Golf Club,** 3807 75th St. W. (☎ **941/792-7476**), just north of Fla. 684 and east of Palma Sola Bay, with an 18-hole, par-72 course and the same 2-day advance booking requirement.

Situated just off U.S. 41, the **Heather Hills Golf Club,** 101 Cortez Rd. W. (☎ **941/755-8888**), operates an 18-hole, par-61 executive course on a first-come, first-served basis. There's a driving range, and clubs can be rented. It's open daily from 6:30am until dark.

Bradenton also is home to the well-known **David Leadbetter Golf Academy,** 1414 69th Ave. (at U.S. 41) (☎ **800/424-3542** or 941/739-2483; www.leadbetter.com), a part of the Nick Bollettieri Sports Academy (see "Tennis," below). Presided over by one of golf's leading instructors, this facility offers practice tee instruction, video analysis, and scoring strategy, as well as general tuition.

KAYAKING

Native Rentals, in S&S Plaza, 5340 Marina Dr., opposite the BP service station in Holmes Beach (☎ **941/778-7757**), rents one- and two-person kayaks and has guided tours around the mangrove islands dotting some of the bay near here. Rentals start at $8 an hour, $24 a day. Guided tours begin at $24 per person. Call for details about the tours.

SPECTATOR SPORTS

The **Pittsburgh Pirates** do their February-through-March spring training at 6,562-seat McKechnie Field, 9th Street West and 17th Avenue West (☎ **941/748-4610**), south of downtown Bradenton. Admission ranges from $6 to $9.

TENNIS

The **Nick Bollettieri Sports Academy,** 5500 34th St. W. (☎ **800/872-6425** or 941/755-1000; www.bollettieri.com/sports/sports.html), is one of the world's largest tennis-training facilities, with more than 70 championship courts and a pro shop. It's open year-round, and reservations are required for all activities. The academy also has training courses in soccer, baseball, and golf.

5 Exploring the Area

On weekends, you can see the sights of rural Manatee County northwest of Bradenton on a 1$\frac{1}{4}$-hour narrated sightseeing tour aboard a 1950s diesel-engine train operated by the **Florida Gulf Coast Railroad,** 83rd Street East, off U.S. 301 in Parrish (☎ **941/722-4272**). The schedule and fares are seasonal, so call before driving out here.

🜚 **DeSoto National Memorial.** DeSoto Memorial Hwy. (north end of 75th St. W.). ☎ **941/792-0458.** Free admission. Daily 9am–5pm. Take Manatee Ave. (Fla. 64) west to 75th St. W. and turn right; follow the road to its end and the entrance to the park.

Nestled on the Manatee River west of downtown, this park re-creates the look and atmosphere of when Spanish explorer Hernando de Soto landed here in 1539. It includes a restoration of de Soto's original campsite and a scenic half-mile nature trail that circles a mangrove jungle and leads to the ruins of one of the first settlements of the area. From December to March, park employees dress in 16th–century costumes and portray the way the early settlers lived, including demonstrations of cooking and musket firing.

Gamble Plantation. 3708 Patten Ave. (U.S. 301), Ellenton. ☎ **941/723-4536.** Free admission. Tours $3 adults, $1.50 children 6–12, free for children under 6. Thurs–Mon 9am–4:30pm; 30-minute guided house tours 9:30 and 10:30am, and 1, 2, 3, and 4pm. Take U.S. 301 north of downtown to Ellenton; the site is on the left just east of Ellenton-Gillette Rd. (Fla. 683).

Situated northeast of downtown Bradenton, this is the oldest structure on the southwestern coast of Florida, and a fine example of an antebellum plantation home. Built over a 6-year period in the late 1840s by Maj. Robert Gamble, it was constructed primarily of "tabby mortar" (a mixture of oyster shells, sand, molasses, and water), with 10 rooms, verandas on 3 sides, 18 exterior columns, and 8 fireplaces. It's maintained as a state historic site and includes a fine collection of 19th–century furnishings. Entrance to the house is by tour only, although you can explore the grounds on your own. The Prime Outlets mall is a 5-minute drive from here, so you can combine a plantation visit with some bargain hunting (see "Shopping," below).

Manatee Village Historical Park. 6th Ave. E. and 15th St. E. ☎ **941/749-7165.** Free admission; donations welcome. Mon–Fri 9am–4:30pm. From downtown, go east on 6th Ave. E. through a merger with Manatee Ave., then right on 15th St. E.

History buffs may enjoy a stroll through this national historic site, a tree-shaded park with a courtyard of hand-laid bricks. Among the restored buildings are the 1860 Manatee County Court House, the oldest structure of its kind still standing on the south Florida mainland; a Methodist church built in 1887; a typical "Cracker Gothic" dating from 1912; and the 1903 Wiggins General Store, full of local memorabilia from swamp root and grub dust to louse powder.

⭐ **South Florida Museum.** Bishop Planetarium, and Parker Manatee Aquarium. 201 10th St. W. (on the riverfront, at Barcarrota Blvd.). ☎ **941/746-4131.** Admission $7.50 adults, $6 seniors, $4 children 5–12, free for children 4 and under. Admission includes planetarium shows. Jan–Apr and July, Mon–Sat 10am–5pm, Sun noon–5pm. Rest of year, Tues–Sat 10am–5pm, Sun noon–5pm. Closed New Year's Day, Thanksgiving, Christmas. From U.S. 41, take Manatee Ave. west to 10th St. W. and turn right.

If you haven't seen manatees in the wild, the star at this downtown complex is "Snooty," the oldest manatee born in captivity (1948) and Manatee County's official mascot. Snooty lives in the Parker Manatee Aquarium. The South Florida Museum tells the story of Florida's history, from prehistoric times to the present, including a Native American collection with life-size dioramas and a Spanish courtyard containing replicas of 16th–century buildings. The Bishop Planetarium features a 50-foot hemispherical dome that arcs above a seating area, for laser light and educational star shows.

6 Shopping

For discount shopping, the focal point of the Bradenton area is the **Prime Outlets Ellenton,** on U.S. 301 at exit 43 off I-75 in Ellenton (☎ **941/723-1150**), about a 15-minute drive northeast of downtown (turn left at the first stoplight east of I-75). This Spanish-style outdoor center has more than 100 factory and outlet stores, including a Saks Off Fifth Avenue, Coach Leather, Liz Claiborne, Bass Shoes, Corning Revere, Jockey, Levi's, Nike, Ann Taylor, Donna Karan, Jones New York, Paul Harris, DKNY, Tommy Hilfiger, Geoffrey Beene, Van Heusen, Maidenform, Royal Doulton, Mikasa, Seiko, Sony, and Bose. Shops are open Monday to Saturday from 10am to 9pm and Sunday from 11am to 6pm. A free trolley runs around this sprawling complex Tuesday to Sunday from noon to 6pm.

7 Where to Stay

The Bradenton Area Convention and Visitors Bureau (see "Orientation," above) operates a free **reservation service** (☎ **800/4-MANATEE**), and its annual visitor guide lists all of Manatee County's accommodations, including condominium complexes. The bureau also publishes a list of Superior Small Lodgings, clean and comfortable properties with no more than 50 rooms (see "Tips on Accommodation" in chapter 1).

A Paradise Rental Management, 5201 Gulf Dr., Holmes Beach, FL 34217 (☎ **800/237-2252** or 941/778-4800; fax 941/778-7090; www.aparadiserentals.com), represents a number of condo complexes.

Except for those near I-75 east of the city, Bradenton has few national chain motels. On the other hand, those on U.S. 41 and University Parkway near the Sarasota-Bradenton International Airport are about halfway between downtown and Sarasota. On Longboat Key, the Hilton and Holiday Inn are equally convenient to Anna Maria Island and Bradenton. See "Where to Stay," in chapter 5 for details about nearby Sarasota accommodations. The high season here is January to April. Hotel tax is 9% in Manatee County.

ANNA MARIA ISLAND

Anna Maria's lone chain motel is the moderately priced **Econo Lodge Surfside,** 2502 Gulf Dr. N. (at 25th St. N.), Bradenton Beach, FL 34217 (☎ **800/55-ECONO** or 941/778-6671; fax 941/778-0360). This clean and well maintained beachfront facility has 18 suites and 36 spacious rooms in its main three-story building, plus 18 rooms in another building on the beach and 5 more across the street (the latter are the least expensive). Rooms range from $99 to $170 double in winter, $88 to $130 double off-season.

MODERATE

The Beach Inn. 101 66th St., Holmes Beach, FL 34217. ☎ **800/823-2247** or 941/778-9597. Fax 941/778-8303. www.thebeachinn.com. 14 units. A/C TV TEL. Winter $119–$199 double. Off-season $79–$179 double. Rates include continental breakfast. MC, V.

Jo and Frank Davis, owners of the Harrington House (see below), have given this two-story beachfront motel a thorough remodeling and turned it into a couples-oriented inn. The property has two buildings: one on the beach and the other rear facing to a tropical courtyard. Beachfront rooms have fireplaces, raised Jacuzzi tubs, bar areas, small microwaves, king-size beds, shower-only bathrooms, and either balconies or spacious decks separated from the gulf by sea oats. The less expensive units in the rear building are less well equipped; they have two full-size beds. Bungalows and apartments in other buildings are available, too. There's no restaurant here, but guests receive complimentary continental breakfast, and the excellent Beach Bistro (see below) is next door.

Bungalow Beach Resort. 2000 Gulf Dr. N. (between 17th and 22nd aves.), Bradenton Beach, FL 34217. ☎ **800/779-3601** or 941/778-3600. Fax 941/778-1764. www.bungalowbeach.com. 15 units. A/C TV TEL. Winter $140–$250 double. Off-season $90–$165 double. AE, MC, V.

If you want an Old Florida–style bungalow by the beach, owners Bert and Gayle Luper have them at this little complex. In fact, white sand walkways join the beach to these bright and airy clapboard cottages, all spiffed up in recent years. Ranging in size from efficiencies to three bedrooms, they all have rattan and wicker tropical furniture, cooking facilities, and a deck or screened porch. A few units have single-person whirlpool bathtubs, and some have shower-only bathrooms. The four choice cottages open to the beach; the largest has a whirlpool bathtub with a steam-maker, a full gourmet kitchen, and a private wrap-around deck. Three others are grouped around an outdoor swimming pool. There is no restaurant on the grounds, but several are within walking distance.

✪ **Harrington House.** 5626 Gulf Dr. (at 58th St.), Holmes Beach, FL 34217. ☎ **888/828-5566** or 941/778-5444. Fax 941/778-0527. www.harringtonhouse.com. 14 units. A/C TV TEL. Winter $129–$249 double. Off-season $129–$179. MC, V.

Flowers will be everywhere and a private beach awaiting when you arrive at Jo and Frank Harris' bed-and-breakfast, the best romantic lovers' getaway hereabouts. In a tree-shaded setting on the beach overlooking the Gulf of Mexico, this three-story coquina-and-rock house was built in 1925 and exudes an Old Florida ambience. The eight bedrooms are individually decorated with antique, wicker, or rattan furnishings. Some units have four-poster or brass beds, and the higher-priced rooms have French doors leading to balconies overlooking the gulf. In addition to the bedrooms in the main house, four rooms are available in the adjacent Spangler Beach House, a remodeled 1940s captain's home, and four more in the nearby Huth House, a low-slung beachside residence (three units here open to an expansive covered lanai facing the beach through a row of Australian pines). All guests enjoy use of the high-ceilinged living room with fireplace, a beachside pool, patio, and complimentary use of bicycles, kayaks, and other sports equipment. No smoking inside here.

✪ **Tropic Isle Inn.** 2103 Gulf Dr. N. (at 22nd St.), Bradenton Beach, FL 34217. ☎ **941/778-1237.** Fax 941/778-7821. www.annamariaisland.com. 15 units. A/C TV TEL. Winter $80–$115. Off-season $55–$80. Weekly rates available. Minimum 1-week rental Feb–Apr. AE, DISC, MC, V.

Owners Bill and Heather Romberger have worked marvels in renovating and upgrading this older motel, across Gulf Drive from its own narrow strip of beach. They installed a high wall along the roadside, behind which you'll find a lushly landscaped courtyard sporting a tin-roof gazebo for lounging and a pool and brick patio for swimming and sunning. Most guest rooms open to the courtyard, and the downstairs units have their own balconies or brick patios behind white fences. Three of the bright and airy units are standard motel rooms. The others are apartments with one or two bedrooms and living areas with kitchens. Some rooms have shower-only bathrooms, so if you want to soak, ask for one with a combination tub-shower. There's a guest laundry. Restaurants are within walking distance. No smoking in the rooms.

Note: The Rombergers may raise their room rates to reflect the recent improvements here. If so, they may include breakfast.

INEXPENSIVE

Rod & Reel Motel. 877 North Shore Dr. (P.O. Box 1939; at Allamanda St.), Anna Maria, FL 34216. ☎ **941/778-2780.** www.rodandreelmotel.com. 10 units. A/C TV. Winter $89–$119. Off-season $60–$90. Minimum 1-week rental Feb–Apr. AE, DISC, MC, V.

Sitting beside the Rod & Reel Fishing Pier on Anna Maria Island's northeastern end, this older but clean and well-maintained motel opens to a sandy beach with a great view of the Skyway Bridge across Tampa Bay. The one-story, L-shaped structure flanks a courtyard with barbecue grills and a big thatch-roof cabana for shady picnics. The two best rooms open directly to the beach, but four others have views across the courtyard to the bay. The units are smallish (as are their 1950s-vintage, shower-only bathrooms), but they are bright, airy, and sport kitchenettes. You can walk out on the pier and have breakfast, lunch, or dinner at the Rod & Reel Pier Restaurant & Snack Bar (see "Where to Dine," below).

8   Where to Dine

ON THE MAINLAND

✪ **Miller's Dutch Kitchen.** 3401 14th St. W. (U.S. 41 Business, at 34th Ave. W.). ☎ **941/746-8253.** Reservations not accepted. Sandwiches $2–$4.50; main courses $6.25–$13. MC, V. Mon–Sat 11am–8pm. Closed Christmas. AMERICAN.

There's a charming treat waiting inside this modern, nondescript brick building among the auto dealers on U.S. 41 Business, for its Pennsylvania Dutch country dining room is surrounded by a balcony, around whose edge chugs a model train. Over the balcony railing you'll see quilts and other handcrafts, all products of Bradenton's Amish community and all very much for sale. Although plain, the food here is as fresh as it gets. The regular American items such as fried shrimp, stuffed flounder, and barbecued pork ribs are augmented by daily Amish specialties such as cabbage rolls and Dutch casserole (noodles, peas, cheese, potatoes, beef, mushrooms, and chicken soup with croutons). Leave room for dessert: You can choose from 20 types of homemade pies. No smoking and no alcohol here.

Twin Dolphin Marina Grill. On The Pier, 1200 1st Ave. W. (north end of 12th St. W.). ☎ **941/748-8087.** Reservations recommended on weekends. Main courses $14–$24. AE, DC, DISC, MC, V. Sun–Thurs 11:30am–9pm, Fri–Sat 11:30am–11pm. FLORIBBEAN.

Commanding views of the Manatee River draws lunch and afterwork crowds to this downtown restaurant housed in a stately Spanish-style landmark building at the foot of 12th Street (Old Main Street) on Memorial Pier. The best bets are the day's fresh catch either grilled, broiled, blackened, bronzed, or jerked Jamaican-style. Regular main courses include crab cakes, grouper Oscar, and a reasonably good rendition of shrimp Provençal. Lighter fare is available outside at **Flipper's Dockside Patio Grill,** a tropical-style bar by the river; it has a light fare menu. There are valet parking and entertainment weekend evenings.

ANNA MARIA ISLAND
EXPENSIVE

✪ **Beach Bistro.** 6600 Gulf Dr. N. (at 66th St.), Holmes Beach. ☎ **941/778-6444.** Reservations recommended. Main courses $22–$40. Tasting menu $45–$65 per person. AE, DC, DISC, MC, V. Daily 5:30–10pm. INTERNATIONAL.

Winner of a Golden Spoon award as one of Florida's 20 best restaurants, Sean Murphy's culinary oasis is Anna Maria Island's top place for fine dining. It sits right beside the beach, offering wide-windowed views of the sparkling gulf waters. Crisp linens, cut crystal, and fresh flowers on every table enhance a romantic ambience and overall elegance. Bistro bouillabaisse made with premium fish, shrimp, scallops, and squid is the signature dish here. Other regular offerings include Floribbean-style grouper— sautéed in a coconut and cashew crust and finished with a red pepper and papaya sauce.

Also excellent, the **Bistro at Island's End,** 10101 Gulf Dr. in Anna Maria (☎ **941/779-2444**), is a sibling of the Beach Bistro. It has live jazz and a late-night menu.

MODERATE

The Beachhouse. 200 Gulf Dr. N. (at Cortez Rd.), Bradenton Beach. ☎ **941/779-2222.** Reservations not accepted but call for preferred seating. Sandwiches $7–$10; main courses $10–$20. AE, DC, DISC, MC, V. Daily 11:30am–10:30pm. AMERICAN.

This large, lively place sits right on Bradenton Beach with a huge open deck and a covered pavilion facing out to the gulf. Even inside, wide windows let in the view. Owned by Ed Chiles, son of the late U.S. senator and Florida governor Lawton Chiles, the Beachhouse offers daily fresh fish specials, including the signature beechnut grouper (with nutty crust in citrus-butter sauce). There's also a good variety of fare, including seafood salads and pastas, crab cakes, fish-and-chips, and broiled steaks. Local musicians play out on the patio most afternoons and evenings.

✪ **Sandbar.** 100 Spring Ave. (east of Gulf Dr.), Anna Maria. ☎ **941/ 778-0444.** Reservations not accepted; call ahead to get on waiting list. Salads and sandwiches $6–$10; main courses $14–$20. AE, DC, DISC, MC, V. Daily 11:30am–10pm. SEAFOOD.

Sitting on the site of the former Pavilion, built in 1913 when people from Tampa and St. Pete took the ferry here, this popular restaurant is perched right on the beach overlooking the gulf. The air-conditioned, knotty-pine dining room offers several traditional as well as innovative preparations of seafood (crab cakes over a roasted pepper sauce, Southwestern-style grouper). The real action here is under the umbrellas on the lively beachside deck, where a menu of appetizers, sandwiches, salads, and platters are served all day and night. Live music makes a party on the deck Monday to Friday nights and on Saturday and Sunday from 1 to 10pm. The inside bar is one of the few I've seen in Florida with no sports TVs.

Inexpensive

❂ **Gulf Drive Café.** 900 Gulf Dr. N. (at 9th St.), Bradenton Beach. ☎ **941/ 778-1919.** Reservations not accepted. Breakfast $3–$6; sandwiches and burgers $4.50–$6; main courses $7–$12. DISC, MC, V. Daily 7am–9:30pm. SEAFOOD.

Locals flock to this bright gulf-side cafe for one of the best bargains on any beach in Florida. With big windows, bentwood cafe chairs with colorful cushions, and lots of hanging plants and ceiling fans, the coral and green dining room opens to a beach-side patio with tables shaded by a trellis (the wait is worth it). The breakfast fare is led by sweet Belgian waffles, which are available all day. You can also order salads, sandwiches, and burgers anytime here, with quiche du jour, Mediterranean seafood pasta, and regular seafood platters joining the show at 4pm.

Rod & Reel Pier Restaurant & Snack Bar. 875 North Shore Dr., Anna Maria. ☎ **941/778-1885.** Reservations not accepted. Breakfast $2.50–$5; sandwiches $3–$8; main courses $6–$10. DISC, MC, V. Daily 7am–10pm. Closed Thanksgiving and Christmas. From Gulf Dr., turn toward the bay on Pine Ave., left at a dead end onto Bay Blvd., right on North Shore Dr. to pier. SEAFOOD.

Sitting out on the Rod & Reel Pier at the north end of the island, this little no-frills fish-camp enjoys a million-dollar view of Tampa Bay, including Egmont Key and the Skyway Bridge on the horizon. The chow is mostly fried or grilled seafood—fish, shrimp, scallops, forgettable crab cakes, and a piled-high combination platter of all of the above. The lone exception, a tasty Mexican-style grouper (sauteed with peppers, onions, and salsa) is by far the best dish here. They will cook your catch, provided you snag it from the pier.

Rotten Ralph's. 902 S. Bay Blvd., Anna Maria. ☎ **941/778-3953.** Reservations not accepted. Sandwiches and burgers $5–$10; main courses $7–$16. DC, DISC, MC, V. Daily 11am–9pm. From Gulf Dr., turn toward the bay on Pine Ave., then right at a dead end to the end of Bay Blvd. SEAFOOD.

On the north end of the island overlooking Bimini Bay, this casual Old Florida–style restaurant has both indoor and outdoor seating right by the boats docked in the Anna Maria Yacht Basin. You can order pots of two dozen steamed oysters, clams, or crabs, or many other seafood choices from fried clam strips to sautéed scallops. Most fall in the moderate category, but you can opt for inexpensive British-style fish-and-chips (the house specialty) or linguini either plain or with chicken, vegetables or shrimp under

marinara or Alfredo sauces. Other choices include Danish baby-
back ribs and Anna Maria chicken (marinated and grilled with a
honey-mustard sauce).

LONGBOAT KEY

✪ **Moore's Stone Crab.** 800 Broadway (at Bayside Dr). ☎ **941/
383-1748.** Reservations not accepted. Sandwiches and salads $6–$10; main
courses $10–$23. DISC, MC, V. Winter daily 11:30am–9:30pm. Off-season
Mon–Fri 4:30–9:30pm, Sat–Sun 11:30am–9:30pm. SEAFOOD.

In Longbeach, the old fishing village on the north end of Longboat Key, this popular bay-front restaurant began in 1967 as an
offshoot of a family seafood business established 40 years earlier.
From the outside, in fact, it still looks a little like a packing house,
but the view of the bay dotted with mangrove islands makes a
fine complement to stone crabs fresh from the family's own traps
from October to March. Otherwise, the menu offers every imag-
inable seafood, most of it fried or broiled. Sandwiches and salads
are served all day.

9   Bradenton & Anna Maria Island After Dark

Locals and visitors alike head south to neighboring Sarasota for
their culture (see "Sarasota After Dark," in chapter 5). Meantime,
the action here is at beach restaurants and pubs.

Live bands lend a party atmosphere to the gulf-side deck at the
Sandbar restaurant every night and from 1pm on weekends (see
"Where to Dine," above). The elegant **Cafe Robar,** at the corner
of Gulf Drive and Pine Avenue in Anna Maria (☎ **941/
778-6969**), offers piano music and a sing-along bar on Tuesday
to Sunday evenings. **D. Coy Ducks Bar & Grille,** in the Island
Shopping Center at Marina Drive and 54th Street in Holmes
Beach (☎ **941/778-5888**), has a varied program of live Dixie-
land bands, jazz pianists, and guitarists.

7

An Excursion to Walt Disney World & Orlando

*L*ocated just and hour east of the Tampa Bay area, a side trip to Walt Disney World and Orlando gives you both a taste of the theme park action and the opportunity to escape the madness at the end of the day (or two).

With so many tourist attractions vying for your time and money, advance planning is a must. Walt's World now encompasses four distinct theme parks, two entertainment districts, enough hotels to fill a small city, and several smaller attractions, including water parks and mini-golf courses. That being said, you'll probably only be visiting for a day or so (if you plan a stay longer than that, a more comprehensive guide, such as *Frommer's Walt Disney World & Orlando* is in order), it's a good idea to pick one or two parks and get to them.

1 Orientation

WHEN TO GO

Since Orlando is essentially a theme-park destination, its busiest seasons are whenever kids are out of school—summer (early June to about Aug 20), holiday weekends, Christmas season (mid-Dec to mid-Jan), and Easter. Obviously, the whole experience is more enjoyable when the crowds are thinnest and the weather is the most temperate. Hotel rooms are also priced lower in the off-season. Best times: the week after Labor Day until Thanksgiving, the week after Thanksgiving until mid-December, and the 6 weeks before and after school spring vacations. Worst times: the week before and after Christmas, and summer when crowds are very large and the weather is oppressively hot and humid.

GETTING THERE
BY CAR

Orlando is 84 miles from Tampa, and the drive, a straight shot on I-4, usually takes a bit less than an hour each way. For car-rental information, see Chapter 1.

BY BUS

Although there is no direct train service between Tampa and Orlando, **Amtrak** (☎ **800/872-7245;** www.amtrak.com) shuttles passengers between Orlando, Tampa, St. Petersburg, and Tarpon Springs via its connecting Thruway bus service. **Greyhound** (☎ **800/231-2222;** www.greyhound.com) also has scheduled bus service between the Tampa Bay area and Orlando.

VISITOR INFORMATION

Contact the **Orlando/Orange County Convention and Visitors Bureau,** 8723 International Dr., Suite 101, Orlando, FL 32819 (☎ **407/363-5871**). The bureau can answer all of your questions and send maps and brochures, such as the *Official Visitors Guide, African-American Visitors Guide, Area Guide* to restaurants, *Official Accommodations Guide,* and *Discover the Unexpected Orlando!* The packet should land in about 3 weeks and include the "Magicard," which is good for up to $500 in discounts on accommodations, car rentals, attractions, and more. If you don't require a human voice, you can order by calling ☎ **800/643-9492** or 800/551-0181.

For general information about **Walt Disney World**—including vacation brochures and videos by age groups—write or call Walt Disney World, Box 10000, Lake Buena Vista, FL 32830-1000 (☎ **407/934-7639**).

If you have Internet access, you can get a ton of other information at WDW's Web site, **www.disneyworld.com**. There's also information available at **www.orlandosentinel.com** and **www.go2orlando.com**.

2　Tips on Visiting Walt Disney World

Walt Disney World is the umbrella for four big-time parks: the Magic Kingdom, Epcot, Disney-MGM Studios, and Animal Kingdom. Besides these major theme parks, Disney has an assortment of other venues, including Downtown Disney Marketplace, Disney West Side (Cirque du Soleil and DisneyQuest, a virtual arcade), Pleasure Island, River Country, Blizzard Beach, Typhoon Lagoon, and more.

For the purposes of this chapter, I've only provided detailed descriptions of the Magic Kingdom, Epcot, and MGM-Studios. For more detailed information on other parks in the area— including Disney's Animal Kingdom, Universal Studios Florida,

Islands of Adventure, and SeaWorld—refer to *Frommer's Walt Disney World & Orlando.*

TIPS FOR PLANNING YOUR TRIP

Advance planning is a must when visiting Walt Disney World. Since you'll be staying a short time, you can't possibly see everything, experience all the rides and attractions, and take advantage of all the recreational facilities. Trying to experience everything will make your visit more of a chore than a vacation and will leave you feeling worn out and miserable.

In order to get the most out of your visit, read the descriptions in this guide and then try and come up with an itinerary that will suit your interests. Make sure to schedule some downtime for yourself—a sit-down lunch or an afternoon swim are good ways to relax—so you leave yourself with some energy to tackle the rest of the afternoon and evening. Also, it's important to have an agreed-upon meeting place in case the family gets separated.

Information   Before leaving home, call or write the Walt Disney World Co., Box 10000, Lake Buena Vista, FL 32830-1000 (☎ **800/828-0228** or 407/934-7639), for a copy of the very informative *Walt Disney World Vacations* brochure—an invaluable planning aid. Once you arrive, there are information booths in each park: In the Magic Kingdom at City Hall, in Epcot at Innoventions East near the World Key, and at Guest Services in Disney-MGM.

Arrive Early   If you want to be first on primo rides at the parks, we suggest you arrive up to 1 hour before opening.

Parking   Parking costs $6 for cars, $7 for RVs. Folks with mobility impairments can park in special lots; call ☎ **407/824-4321.** *Don't forget to write down where you parked;* it's easy to get lost after a long day.

When You Arrive   Grab a guide map! It not only tells you where the fun stuff is, but also lists the day's entertainment schedule. If you want to see certain shows or parades, arrive early to get a good seat. Use this guide and the map to come up with a game plan on where to eat, what to ride, and what to see during your stay.

Best Days to Visit   Generally, the busiest days at all parks are Saturdays and Sundays, when the locals visit. Beyond that: Mondays and Thursdays are frantic in the Magic Kingdom; Tuesdays

---

Time Saver _____

FASTPASS is reservation system in which you go to the primo rides, feed your ticket into a slot, and get an assigned time to return. When you do, you get into a shorter line. You can get only one FASTPASS reservation at a time. While rides change from time to time, FASTPASS is at more than a dozen popular ones in the Magic Kingdom, Epcot, Disney-MGM Studios, and Animal Kingdom.

---

and Fridays are hectic at Epcot; and Wednesdays spell insanity at Disney-MGM Studios.

Operating Hours   They vary through the year and can be influenced by special events, so it's a good idea to call during your visit or earlier to check opening/closing times. Generally, the parks open at 9am and close from 7 to 9pm, although some are open later during summer and other peak periods.

Tickets   A **1-day ticket** to the Magic Kingdom, Epcot, or Disney-MGM costs $46 for adults, $37 for kids 3 to 9. (Ouch!). If you plan on visiting Walt Disney World more than once per year, or for several days at a time, a money-saving pass may be a good option. Call ☎ **407/824-4321** for information. Visitors staying on Disney property may also be eligible for a discounted pass, ask when you reserve your room.

3 The Magic Kingdom

The Magic Kingdom offers 40 attractions plus restaurants and shops in a 107-acre package. Its symbol, Cinderella's Castle, forms the hub of a wheel whose spokes reach to **seven "lands."**

Arriving   From the parking lot, you walk or take a tram, then a ferry or monorail to the entrance. While rides are short, the wait isn't during peak periods, so plan to arrive an hour before the opening bell and be sure to make a note of where you parked.

When you enter, get a guide map. It shows the park's shops, restaurants, and attractions. Also consult the entertainment schedule on it to see what's cooking today. There are parades, musical extravaganzas, fireworks, band concerts, and character appearances.

If you have any questions, most park employees are very knowledgeable, and City Hall, on your left as you enter, is both an information center, and a great spot to meet up with costumed characters. There's a stroller-rental shop just after the turnstiles to your right, and the Kodak Camera Center, near Town Square, takes care of all your photographic needs.

MAIN STREET, USA

Designed to resemble a turn-of-the-20th-century American street (okay, it leads to a 13th-century European castle), this is the gateway to the Kingdom. Don't dawdle on Main Street when you enter the park; leave it for the end of the day when you're heading to your hotel.

Walt Disney World Railroad and Other Main Street Vehicles Guests on a leisurely pace can ride an authentic 1928 steam-powered railroad for a 15-minute tour of the park. Other leisure vehicles include horse-drawn trolleys, jitneys, omnibuses, and fire engines that travel along Main Street.

Main Street Cinema This air-conditioned hexagonal theater features vintage black-and-white Disney 'toons, including 1928's *Steamboat Willie* in which Mickey and Minnie debuted. *Note:* This theater has no seats.

ADVENTURELAND

Cross a bridge and stroll through an exotic jungle of foliage, thatched roofs, and totems. Amid dense vines and stands of bamboo, drums are beating, and swashbuckling adventures are taking place.

✪ **Jungle Cruise** In the course of 10 minutes, you sail through an African veldt in the Congo, an Amazon rain forest, and the Nile in Egypt. There are dozens of animatronic birds, elephants, giraffes, crocodiles, tigers, and butterflies in lavish scenery that includes cascading waterfalls, and tropical foliage. Passengers find themselves threatened by angry elephants and warriors who attack with spears. This is cheesy Disney at its best.

Pirates of the Caribbean You board a fake log and enter a cave. Inside there are hundreds of audio-animatronic figures, from critters to "yo-ho-ho-ing," plundering pirates who raid a Caribbean town. After a lot of looting and boozing, the pirates pass out. This ride might be scary for kids under 5.

Swiss Family Treehouse   This attraction, based on the movie *Swiss Family Robinson,* lets you walk a rope bridge to the adult-size house in a banyan tree built by Disney. The tree has 330,000 polyethylene leaves sprouting from a 90-foot span of branches. *Note:* People with limited mobility beware—there's lots of climbing.

FRONTIERLAND

From Adventureland, step into the wild and woolly past of the American frontier! The landscape is straight out of the Wild West, with log cabins and rustic saloons. Across the river is Tom Sawyer Island, reachable via log rafts.

✪ **Big Thunder Mountain Railroad**   This low-key roller coaster has tight turns and dark descents rather than sudden, steep drops. It's situated in a 200-foot, red-stone mountain with 2,780 feet of track winding through caves and canyons. Your runaway train careens through the ribs of a dinosaur, under a thundering waterfall, past spewing geysers and bubbling mud pots, and over a bottomless volcanic pool.

✪ **Splash Mountain**   Based on the 1946 Disney film, *Song of the South,* Splash Mountain takes you on an enchanting journey in a log craft down a flooded mountain. Riders find themselves caught up in the bumbling schemes of Brer Fox and Brer Bear as they pursue the ever-wily Brer Rabbit through backwoods swamps, bayous, and waterfalls. The music from the film forms a delightful audio backdrop. Your log twists, turns, and splashes, dropping into darkness and a 52-foot, 45° splashdown at 40 m.p.h.

Tom Sawyer Island   Board Huck Finn's raft for a 1-minute float across the river to this densely forested island. Kids love exploring the narrow passages of Injun Joe's cave, a windmill, and an abandoned mine. There's also a rickety swing, barrel bridges, and sit-downs for weary parents. Aunt Polly's restaurant serves fried chicken and PB&Js on outdoor tables with views of the river.

Diamond Horseshoe Saloon Revue & Medicine Show   Enjoy Dr. Bill U. Later's turn-of-the-20th-century Wild West revue. Jingles plays honky-tonk, there's a magic act, Miss Lucille L'Amour and her dance-hall girls do a spirited cancan, and there's a ton of audience participation in seven shows daily.

Frontierland Shootin' Arcade   Fog creeps across the graveyard, coyotes howl, bridges groan, and skeletons rise as state-of-the-art electronics combine with a traditional shooting-gallery format. If you hit the tombstone, it spins and the epitaph changes. Fifty cents buys you 25 shots.

Country Bear Jamboree This hoot is a 15-minute show featuring audio-animatronic bears belting out rollicking country tunes and crooning plaintive love songs. Wisecracking commentary comes from a mounted buffalo, moose, and deer on the wall.

LIBERTY SQUARE

This zone between Frontierland and Fantasyland shows an 18th-century America with colonial architecture. Thirteen lanterns, symbolizing the colonies, hang from the Liberty Tree, an immense live oak. You might encounter a fife-and-drum corps on the cobblestone streets.

Hall of Presidents Every American president is represented by a lifelike audio-animatronic figure. If you look closely, you'll see them fidget and whisper during the performance. The show begins with a film—projected on a 180°, 70mm screen—that talks about the importance of the Constitution. Then the curtain rises on America's leaders, and as each comes into the spotlight, he nods or waves with presidential dignity.

Haunted Mansion Darkness, spooky music, eerie howling, and mysterious screams and rappings enhance this spot's ambience. The ride is replete with bizarre scenes and objects: a ghostly banquet and ball, a graveyard band, a suit of armor that comes alive, luminous spiders, a talking head in a crystal ball, and weird flying objects. At the end of the ride, a ghost joins you in your car. The experience is more amusing than terrifying, so you can take small children inside.

Boat Rides A steam-powered sternwheeler, the *Liberty Belle,* and one or two Mike Fink keelboats depart Liberty Square for scenic cruises along the Rivers of America. Both ply the same route and make a restful interlude for foot-weary park-stompers.

FANTASYLAND

The attractions in this happy land are themed after classics such as *Snow White, Peter Pan,* and *Dumbo.* They're very popular with young visitors. If your kids are 8 and under, you may want to make this and Mickey's Toontown your first stops in the Magic Kingdom.

Cinderella's Castle   There's not a lot to do, but its status as the Magic Kingdom's icon makes it a must. This fairyland castle with 185-foot-high Gothic spires is situated at the end of Main Street, directly in the center of the park. The namesake character appears sometimes, and Cinderella's Royal Table, the restaurant, is inside.

Cinderella's Golden Carousel   This beauty was constructed by Italian carvers in 1917, and refurbished by Disney artists who added 18 hand-painted scenes from Cinderella on a wooden canopy above the horses. The carousel organ plays Disney classics such as "When You Wish Upon a Star."

Dumbo, the Flying Elephant   This is a very tame kid ride in which cars that are Dumbo clones go around in a circle, gently rising and dipping. If you can stand the lines, it's very exciting for wee ones and adults who are thrilled when they are.

It's a Small World   If you don't know the song, you will by the end of the ride. It'll crawl into your mind like a brain-eating mite, playing continually as you sail "around the world." All of the countries you meet are inhabited by appropriately costumed animatronic dolls incessantly singing "It's a small world after all" in tiny doll-like voices. Adults have to pay their dues and ride this one at least once.

Legend of the Lion King   This stage show is based on Disney's motion-picture musical and combines animation, movie footage, sophisticated puppetry, and high-tech special effects. The show is enhanced by the music of Elton John and Tim Rice. Actors providing voices include Whoopi Goldberg and Cheech Marin.

Mad Tea Party   Alice in Wonderland is the theme of this traditional amusement-park ride. Riders sit in big pastel teacups on saucers that careen around a circular platform, spinning either fast or slow depending on the nausea tolerance of occupants, who spin a wheel.

The Many Adventures of Winnie the Pooh   The Many Adventures of Winnie the Pooh features the cute-and-cuddly little fellow, along with pals Eyeore, Piglet, and Tigger. You board a golden honey pot and ride through a storybook version of the Hundred-Acre Wood, keeping an eye out for Heffalumps, Woozles, and Blustery Days.

Peter Pan's Flight   Riding in airborne versions of Captain Hook's ship, passengers careen through dark passages while experiencing the story of Peter Pan. The adventure begins in the Darlings' nursery and includes a flight over nighttime London to Never-Never Land. There, riders encounter mermaids, Indians, a ticking crocodile, the Lost Boys, Princess Tiger Lilly, Tinker Bell, Hook, and Smee, all to the theme, "You Can Fly, You Can Fly, You Can Fly." It's fun.

Snow White's Scary Adventures   Snow White appears in several pleasant scenes, such as at the wishing well and riding away with the prince to live happily ever after. There are new audio-animatronic dwarfs, and the colors have been brightened and made less threatening than in the ride's original incarnation. Even so, this could be scary for kids under 5.

MICKEY'S TOONTOWN FAIR

Head off those cries of "Where's Mickey?" by taking young kids to this 2-acre site. Toontown lets them meet their favorite Disney characters, including Mickey, Minnie, Donald, Goofy, and Pluto. The kingdom's smallest land is set in a whimsical collection of candy-striped tents like those long-gone county fairs. **The Barnstormer at Goofy's Wiseacres Farm** is a mini—roller coaster made to look like a crop duster that flies off course and through Goofy's barn. **Donald's Boat** is an interactive fountain with enough surprises to win squeals of joy (and relief on hot days). **Minnie's Country House** gives kids a chance to play in her kitchen, while **Mickey's Country House** has garden and garage playgrounds, plus a chance to meet the big cheese himself. And **Mickey's Toontown Hall of Fame** offers continuous meetings with Disney favorites.

TOMORROWLAND

In 1994, the WDW folks decided Tomorrowland (originally designed in the 1970s) was beginning to look like "Yesteryear." The section was revamped to show the future as a galactic, science fiction–inspired community inhabited by humans, aliens, and robots. A state-of-the-art video-game arcade was also added.

✪ **ExtraTERRORestrial Alien Encounter**   *Star Wars* director George Lucas was paid to add his space-age vision to this attraction. It begins with a mysterious interplanetary corporation called X-S Tech, selling tele-transporter services—you can beam between planets light years apart—to Earthlings like you. X-S technicians try to teleport their sinister corporation head, Chairman Clench, to Earth. But the machine malfunctions, sending Clench instead to a distant planet and, inadvertently, teleporting a fearsome extraterrestrial to Earth. This virtual ride/show carries a legitimate child warning about being dark, scary, and confining (the shoulder plate locks you in). It delivers high-tech effects, from the alien's breath on your neck to a mist of alien slime.

Astro Orbiter This tame amusement-park ride could have come from your county fair. The "rockets" are on arms attached to "the center of the galaxy," and they move up and down while orbiting planets. The line tends to move slowly, so unless it's short, skip this one.

Buzz Lightyear's Space Ranger Spin Join Buzz in a fight to save the universe while flying your own joystick-controlled cruiser through a world you'll recognize from the movie *Toy Story.* The kids enjoy using the laser cannons as they spin through space (filled with gigantic toys). If you're a good shot, you can set off sight and sound gags with these light lasers. A display in the car keeps the shooter's score, so take multiple cars if you have more than one child.

✪ Space Mountain While you wait in line, Space Mountain entertains you with space-age music and exhibits, as meteorites, shooting stars, and space debris whiz overhead. These illusioneering effects continue during the ride—a cosmic roller coaster in the inky, starlit blackness of outer space. Your rocket climbs high into the universe before racing through a serpentine complex of aerial galaxies, making thrilling hairpin turns and rapid plunges. (It feels like warp speed, but your car never goes faster than 28 m.p.h.) Nab the front seat of the train for the best ride.

The Timekeeper This Jules Verne/H. G. Wells–inspired multimedia presentation combines CircleVision and IMAX footage with audio-animatronics. It's hosted by Timekeeper, a mad-scientist robot (Robin Williams) and his assistant, 9-EYE, a flying, camera-headed 'droid and time-machine test pilot. In this jet-speed escapade, the audience hears Mozart as a young prodigy playing his music to French royalty, visits medieval battlefields in Scotland, watches da Vinci work, and floats in a hot-air balloon above Moscow's Red Square.

Tomorrowland Speedway This can be fun for the very young. The cars go real slow and are on a loose track, even though they're actual gas-powered mini–sports cars. Maximum speed on the

4-minute drive around the track is 7 m.p.h., and kids have to be 52 inches tall to drive alone. Teens and childless adults will probably be bored.

Tomorrowland Transit Authority   A futuristic means of transportation, these small five-car trains have no engines. They work by electromagnets, emit no pollution, and use little power. They offer an overhead look at Tomorrowland, including a pretty good interior view of Space Mountain. If you're in the Magic Kingdom for only 1 day, skip this. If you're looking for a little snooze cruise, it's a must.

Walt Disney's Carousel of Progress   Apologies to its fans, but this 22-minute ride/show takes up too much time for its limited wow power. Though refurbished in 1993, it's still in the 1930s—where the show begins—in terms of amusement and modern rides.

PARADES, FIREWORKS & MORE

Consult your map for the entertainment schedule for concerts, character encounters, holiday events, and the three major happenings below.

Disney's Magical Moments Parade   With relatively few floats, all showcasing Disney movies, your interest in this parade will depend on how much time you're willing to take away from the attractions. The parade includes lots of dancers and extras. If you're on a tight schedule, skip it and go to one of the primo rides while the masses flock here.

✪ **The Main Street Electrical Parade**   This Disney favorite, which ran for 20 years at Walt Disney World before moving to Disneyland in 1991, has been brought back with the same floats and costumes used recently at Disneyland. (Its WDW predecessor, Spectromagic, has been sent to Disneyland Paris.) Show times vary with seasons. The 20-minute **Electrical Parade** is held every night during summer and other peak times, Thursday through Saturday in the off-season.

Fireworks   Fantasy in the Sky is an explosive fireworks display. Disney has pyrotechnics down to an art and this is a great way to end the day. Fantasy in the Sky takes place nightly during summer and holidays, on selected nights the rest of the year. Consult your entertainment schedule for details. Suggested viewing areas are Liberty Square, Frontierland, and Mickey's Toontown Fair. Disney hotels close to the park also offer excellent views.

4 Epcot

This 260-acre theme park is so stunningly landscaped, it's worth visiting for its botanical beauty alone. There are two major sections—Future World and World Showcase.

Epcot is large and walking around it can be exhausting. Though we really don't recommend it—park veterans not-so-jokingly maintain that Epcot stands for "Every Person Comes Out Tired"—it is possible to do the park in a single day. Conserve your energy by taking launches across the lagoon from the edge of Future World to Germany or Morocco. Double-decker buses circle World Showcase, making stops at Norway, Italy, France, and Canada.

FUTURE WORLD

Centered on a giant geosphere known as Spaceship Earth, Future World encompasses 10 themed areas sponsored by major corporations. Attractions focus on discovery, scientific achievements, and tomorrow's technologies in areas running from energy to undersea exploration. This area has most of Epcot's theme park–style rides.

Spaceship Earth This giant golf ball–like sphere is Epcot's icon, but as rides go it's a real snoozer. The 15-minute journey takes visitors to the distant past, where an audio-animatronic Cro-Magnon shaman recounts the story of a hunt while others record it on cave walls. Then you advance through thousands of years of communications. During the Renaissance, you may notice that several beings look an awful lot like Barbie's dream date, Ken.

Test Track Test Track is a long-time-in-coming marvel that combines GM engineering and Disney imagineering. The line can be more than an hour long in peak periods, so think FAST-PASS. The last part of the line passes displays on corrosion, crash tests, and more. The 5-minute ride follows what looks to be an actual highway. You'll endure braking tests, a hill climb, and tight s-curves while seated in a six-passenger "convertible." There's also a 12-second burst of speed on a straightaway and a loop that gets your heart pumping to the tune of 65 m.p.h. *Tip:* The left front seat has the most thrills in the curves.

Innoventions Just beyond Spaceship Earth, this pair of crescent-shaped buildings—located on both your right and your left—include 100,000 square feet of exhibit space showcasing cutting-edge technology and future products. Revised in 1999 for the millennium, Innoventions uses Disney Channel robot host Tom Morrow 2.0 to greet guests and lead the way through nine exhibits. These include radiology's 3-D body images, a 30-by-80-foot high-definition TV screen, an area where you can create video e-mail to send to your friends, and lessons about future forestry, agriculture, and digital-information sharing. Many of the areas have hands-on, interactive exhibits and games. The best in this realm is Video Games of Tomorrow, sponsored by Sega. Its 34 play stations give you a look at the future of video games and let you participate in a "motion-capture shoot" that translates body movements into a digital, game-style playback.

The two-story **Discovery Center,** located on the right side of Innoventions, includes an information resource area where guests can get answers to their questions about Epcot attractions in particular, and Walt Disney World in general.

The Living Seas   This pavilion has a 5.7-million-gallon saltwater aquarium with a coral reef inhabited by 4,000 sea creatures. While waiting in line, visitors pass exhibits tracing the history of undersea exploration. A $2^1/_2$-minute multimedia preshow about today's ocean technology is followed by a 7-minute film demonstrating the formation of the earth and seas as a means to support life.

After the films, visitors enter hydrolators for a rapid "descent" to the ocean floor. Upon arrival, they board Seacabs that wind around a 400-foot-long tunnel to enjoy stunning close-up views through acrylic windows of ocean denizens in a natural coral-reef habitat. The ride concludes at the Seabase Concourse, which is the visitor center of **Seabase Alpha,** a prototype ocean-research facility of the future. Here, exhibits include a $22^1/_2$-foot scuba tube used by Seabase Alpha scientists to enter and leave the water. There also are seven information modules containing numerous exhibits on ocean ecosystems, marine mammals, the study of oceanography from space, and undersea exploration. Many of these exhibits are hands-on. You can step into a diver's JIM Suit and use controls to complete diving tasks and expand your knowledge of oceanography via interactive computers. The Living Seas also has two manatees living in too-tight quarters.

The Land   This largest of Future World's pavilions highlights our relation to food and nature.

Living with the Land is a 13-minute boat ride through three ecological environments (a rain forest, an African desert, and the windswept American plains), each populated by appropriate audio-animatronic denizens. New farming methods and experiments, ranging from hydroponics to plants growing in simulated Martian soil, are showcased in real gardens.

Circle of Life combines spectacular live-action footage with animation in a 15-minute 70mm movie based on *The Lion King.* In this environmental tale, Timon and Pumbaa want to build Hakuna Matata Lakeside Village, but, as Simba points out, their project is damaging the habitat of other animals. The message: Everything is connected in the great circle of life.

In **Food Rocks,** audio-animatronic rock performers deliver an entertaining message on nutrition.

Journey Into Imagination   This pavilion offers several venues, but don't miss the fountains with water that leaps like glass rods—the kids will love trying to catch them.

The 3-D **Honey, I Shrunk the Audience** ride is the headliner here. Based on the Disney hit *Honey, I Shrunk the Kids* film, you're first terrorized by mice and, once you're shrunk, a large cat; then you're given a good shaking by a gigantic 5-year-old. Vibrating seats and creepy tactile effects enhance dramatic 3-D action. Finally, everyone returns to proper size—everyone, that is, but the family dog, which creates the final, not altogether expected surprise.

Wonders of Life   Housed in a vast geodesic dome fronted by a 75-foot replica of a DNA strand, this pavilion offers some of Future World's most engaging shows and attractions.

✪ **Body Wars:** You're reduced to the size of a cell for a medical rescue mission. Your objective: Save a miniaturized immunologist who was accidentally sucked into a patient's bloodstream. This motion-simulator ride takes you through gale-force winds in the lungs and heart chambers. *Tip:* If you like being tossed around, engineers designed the ride from the last row of a car, so that's where it's bumpiest.

Cranium Command: In this hilarious, multimedia presentation, Buzzy, an audio-animatronic brain-pilot-in-training, is charged with the seemingly impossible task of controlling the brain of a typical 12-year-old boy. You'll tag along with this would-be Cranium Commando as a gruff, but good-hearted drill-sergeant helps whip Buzzy into shape.

The Making of Me: This short film stars Martin Short, who gives a tasteful description of conception and birth that's suitable even for 10- to 12-year-olds.

Universe of Energy The solar panels on its roof are a clue to the theme: Making you better understand America's energy problems and solutions. Its 32-minute ride, **Ellen's Energy Adventure,** features comedian Ellen DeGeneres as an energy expert tutored by Bill Nye the Science Guy to be a *Jeopardy!* contestant. You travel from Earth's beginnings to the formation of fossil fuels. In the Mesozoic Era, you'll find a time of violent geological activity and be confronted by audio-animatronic dragonflies, pterodactyls, and dinosaurs. Zapped back to the present, you'll enter a NASA Mission Control Room, where you'll see a film on how energy affects our lives. The ride ends on an upbeat note, with a vision of an energy-abundant future, and Ellen as a new *Jeopardy!* champion.

WORLD SHOWCASE

This community of 11 miniaturized nations surrounds a 40-acre lagoon at Epcot's south end. All of the Showcase's countries have authentically indigenous landmarks, landscaping, background music, restaurants, and shops. Cultural facets are explored in artworks, dance performances, and innovative rides, films, and attractions. The employees in each pavilion are natives of that country.

You can indulge in a plethora of international experience here: down a pint in an authentic British pub, sail the Norwegian fjords in a Viking longship, or watch a demonstration of Chinese calligraphy. Countries represented at the World Showcase include Mexico, China, Italy, Germany, Morocco, Norway, Japan, France, the United Kingdom, Canada, and the United States. For details on some of the restaurants in this section of the park, refer to the "Where to Dine" section at the end of this chapter.

SHOWS & SPECTACULARS

As in the Magic Kingdom, guide maps and show schedules are available as soon as you enter the park.

IllumiNations Those who arrive before January 1, 2001, will see the millennium version, IllumiNations 2000, though in our opinion one is as good as the other. This is a grand nightcap—a blend of fireworks, lasers, and fountains in a display that's signature

Disney. The show is well worth the crowds that flock to the parking lot at its conclusion. *Tip:* This is a very popular show and draws a lot of people, but there are tons of good viewing points around the lagoon. Still, it's best to stake your claim to a primo place to park your fanny a half hour or so before show time, which is listed in your entertainment schedule.

Other Shows Live shows, especially those in the World Showcase, make up an important part of the Epcot experience. These performances might include Chinese lion dancers and acrobats, German oompah bands, Caledonian bagpipers, Mexican mariachi bands, Moroccan storytellers and belly dancers, Italian "living statues" and stilt walkers, colonial fife and drum corps, and more. Two especially good shows are the Voices of Liberty singers at the American Adventure pavilion and the traditional music and dance displays in Japan. Check your guide map/show schedule when you come in.

5 Disney-MGM Studios

You'll probably spy the Tower of Terror and the Earrfel Tower, a water tower with mouse ears, before you enter this park, which Disney bills as "the Hollywood that never was and always will be." Once inside, you'll find pulse-quickening rides such as Rock 'n' Roller Coaster, movie- and TV-themed shows, and behind-the-scenes "reel-life" adventures.

✪ **The Twilight Zone Tower of Terror** This is a truly stomach-lifting ride and Disney continues to fine-tune it to make it better. Its legend says that during a violent storm on Halloween night 1939, lightning struck the Hollywood Tower Hotel, causing an entire wing and an elevator full of people to disappear. And you're about to meet them as you star in a special episode of . . . *The Twilight Zone.* Eerie corridors lead to a dimly lit library, where you can hear a storm raging outside. After various spooky adventures, the ride ends in a dramatic climax: a terrifying, 13-story free-fall into *The Twilight Zone!* For some this is the best thrill ride anywhere in Disney.

✪ **Voyage of the Little Mermaid** Hazy lighting in a reef-walled theater creates an underwater effect and helps set the mood for this charming musical based on the Disney feature film. The show combines live performers with more than 100 puppets, movie clips, and innovative special effects.

✪ **Indiana Jones Epic Stunt Spectacular**   The world of movie stunts is explored in this dramatic 30-minute show, which re-creates major scenes from the Indiana Jones series. The show opens on an elaborate Mayan temple as Indy crashes onto the set via rope and searches for a golden idol. He encounters booby traps and is chased by a giant boulder! The set is then dismantled to reveal a colorful Cairo marketplace where a sword fight ensues. The action includes bullwhip maneuvers, lots of gunfire, and a truck bursting into flame. An explosive finale takes place in a desert scenario.

✪ **Jim Henson's Muppet*Vision 3D**   This attraction stars Kermit and Miss Piggy in a delightful marriage of Jim Henson's puppets and Disney's audio-animatronics, special-effects wizardry, 70mm film, and cutting-edge 3-D technology. Wow! It's the best of the 3-D films at Disney, and the in-your-face action includes flying Muppets, cannonballs, wind, fiber-optic fireworks, bubble showers, and even an actual spray of water. Kermit is the host, Miss Piggy sings, and Statler and Waldorf critique the action from a balcony. Kids in the first row get to interact with the cast. The 25-minute show runs continuously.

The Magic of Disney Animation   You'll see Disney characters come alive at the stroke of a brush or pencil as you tour glass-walled animation studios. Walter Cronkite and Robin Williams explain what's going on via video monitors and star in an 8-minute Peter Pan–themed film about the basics of animation. It's painstaking work: To produce an 80-minute movie, the animation team must do more than one million drawings of characters and scenery! Original cels (paintings or drawings on celluloid sheets) from famous Disney movies and some of the many Oscars won by Disney artists are on display. The 35-minute tour also includes a selection of magical moments from Disney's classic films.

✪ **Rock 'n' Roller Coaster**   This inverted roller coaster is one of the best thrill rides WDW has to offer. It's a fast-and-furious indoor ride that puts you in a 24-passenger "stretch limo" outfitted with 120 speakers that blare Aerosmith at 32,000 watts! A flashing light warns you to "prepare to merge as you've never merged before," and faster than you can scream "Oh, no!" (around 2.8 seconds, actually), you shoot from 0 to 60 m.p.h. and into the first gut-tightening inversion at 5Gs. It's a real launch (sometimes of lunch) followed by a wild ride through a make-believe California freeway system.

Sounds Dangerous Starring Drew Carey   Actor Drew Carey provides the laughs while dual audio technology provides some incredible hair-raising effects during this 12-minute show at ABC Sound Studios. You'll feel like you're right in the middle of the action in a TV pilot featuring undercover police work and plenty of amusing mishaps. In 1999, Drew replaced Disney's Saturday Morning at ABC Sound Studio.

Star Tours   Cutting edge when it first opened, this galactic journey based on the original *Star Wars* trilogy is a rung below the latest technology, but still a ton of fun. Once inside, you board a 40-seat "spacecraft" for an other-worldly journey that greets you with sudden drops, violent crashes, and oncoming laser blasts as it careens out of control. This is another of those virtual rides where you go nowhere but it feels like you do.

Hunchback of Notre Dame: A Musical Adventure   This rollicking stage show brings the animated feature's main characters to life, mainly with actors but sometimes with puppets. Dozens of performers tell the story of Quasimodo, who was banished to a church bell tower. Show up 30 minutes early to ensure a good seat and at least 5 minutes early for one at all during busy seasons, when the theater sometimes fills to capacity.

The Great Movie Ride   Film footage and 50 audio-animatronic replicas of movie stars are used to re-create some of the most famous scenes in filmdom on this 22-minute ride through movie history. Grown-ups will enjoy this one for two reasons: You get to sit down and you relive magic moments from the 1930s to the present. Kids may be bored until they get to Sigourney Weaver fending off slimy alien foes. The action is enhanced by special effects, and your tram is hijacked en route by outlaws.

Disney's Doug Live   This 30-minute show, one of the park's newest, combines live performers and animation while telling the story of a 12-year-old and his interaction with the popular television cartoon character. This is a must-see for fans of the show, who during audience-participation segments answer Doug trivia faster than you can say "The Evil Dr. Rubber Suit." The show requires four adult volunteers (to play The Beets) and one child (as Quail Man). The music is good and, in summer, the air-conditioning is a blessing.

Beauty and the Beast Live on Stage   The 1,500-seat covered amphitheater is the home of a 25-minute, live Broadway-style production of *Beauty and the Beast* that was adapted from the movie version. Musical highlights from the show include the rousing "Be Our Guest" opening number and the poignant title song, featured in a romantic waltz-scene finale. A highlight is "The Mob Song" scene in a dark forest. Sets and costumes are lavish, and the production numbers are spectacular. Arrive early to get a good seat.

Bear in the Big Blue House—Live on Stage!   Younger audiences will like meeting Bear, Ojo, Tutter, Treelo, Pip, Pop, and Luna as they perform some of their favorite songs from the whimsical Disney Channel series. The 15-minute show is held six times a day.

✪ **Disney-MGM Studios Backlot Tour**   A tram takes you on a 35-minute behind-the-scenes tour for a close-up look at the vehicles, props, costumes, sets, and special effects used in movies and TV shows. You'll see costume makers at work in the wardrobe department, house facades of *The Golden Girls* and *Empty Nest* on Residential Street, and carpenters building sets. The real fun begins once the tram ventures into Catastrophe Canyon, where an earthquake causes a raging oil fire, massive explosions, torrents of rain, and flash floods. Then you're taken behind the scenes to see how filmmakers create such disasters.

Backstage Pass   Have a De Vil of a good time spotting Cruella and the other stars of Disney's live-action remake of *101 Dalmations* during a 25-minute walking tour. The stark, eerie sets from Cruella's movie are among the top attractions during this short tour. Wizzer, the most fluid of the canine actors, is featured in a film about the life of a four-pawed star.

The American Film Institute Showcase   Created in 1996 in partnership with the Los Angeles–based American Film Institute, this walk-through tour also highlights some of the organization's winners of the Lifetime Achievement Award. They include Bette Davis, Jack Nicholson, and Elizabeth Taylor. There are also periodically changing exhibits, such as "Creatures of Distinction," which features puppets, models, and miniatures that play important roles in *Star Wars, Armageddon,* and other movies.

PARADES, SHOWS, FIREWORKS & MORE

Mulan is a parade honoring Disney's 36th full-length animated feature. It's performed afternoons (weather permitting) along Hollywood Boulevard. This parade doesn't touch Magic Kingdom parades in size and scope, so unless you're a big *Mulan* fan, this is a good time to find shorter lines at popular rides such as Tower of Terror or Rock 'n' Roller Coaster.

✪ **Fantasmic!** is an end-of-the-day visual feast of laser lights, fireworks, shooting comets, great balls of fire, and the Magic Mickey. The 25-minute show includes 50 performers, a giant dragon, a king cobra, and 1 million gallons of water, just about all of which are orchestrated by a sorcerer mouse that looks more than remotely familiar. Check your schedule for time. *Tip:* The ample amphitheater holds 9,000 souls, so be prepared to wait to get in, or come late and try your luck at last-minute seating.

6   Where to Stay

The following is just a small selection of hotels in the Orlando area, in case you decide to stay in town for more than 1 day. What follows is just a basic description of each hotel, no dining or amenities listings, so for more information you should contact the hotels directly, or refer to *Frommer's Walt Disney World & Orlando*.

Consider the cost of parking or shuttle buses to and from Disney and other theme parks when making your hotel choice—it can add up to quite a bit. Also, remember to factor in the 11% hotel tax when figuring hotel costs.

WALT DISNEY WORLD CENTRAL RESERVATIONS OFFICE

To reserve a room at Disney hotels, resorts, and villas; official hotels; or Fort Wilderness homes and campsites, contact **WDW Travel Company** at ☎ **800/327-2996** or 800/647-7900 to book single rooms or resort packages. You also can contact **Central Reservations Operations** (CRO), P.O. Box 10000, Lake Buena Vista, FL 32830-1000 (☎ **407/934-7639**).

Both **CRO** and **WDW Travel Company** can recommend accommodations suited to your price range and specific needs. Be sure to inquire about Disney's numerous package plans, which can include meals, tickets, recreation, and other features. All

WDW properties offer handicap-accessible accommodations and special nonsmoking rooms.

You can also check out Disney's various resorts, and reserve a room or vacation package, on Disney's official Web site at **www.disneyworld.com**.

DISNEY RESORTS
VERY EXPENSIVE

✪ **Disney's Grand Floridian Beach Resort.** 4401 Floridian Way (P.O. Box 10000), Lake Buena Vista, FL 32830-1000. ☎ **407/934-7639** or 407/824-3000. Fax 407/824-3186. 933 units. A/C MINIBAR TV TEL. $304–$480 double; $420–$665 concierge levels; $550–$670 concierge deluxe; $690–$1,995 suites. AE, MC, V. Free self- and valet parking.

This is Disney's Flagship resort. From the moment you step into its Great Gatsbyian-style, five-story domed lobby, you'll notice its overabundant Victorian theme. In the afternoons, tea is served to live piano music. In the evenings, an orchestra plays big-band tunes. The hotel's a romantic choice for couples, including honeymooners. You'll find a first-rate health club and spa. The rooms are large and sunny, with private balconies or verandahs overlooking formal gardens, the pool, or a 200-acre lagoon. All rooms come with two queen-size beds or one king-size bed; some have lovely two-poster beds with floral-chintz spreads. In-room amenities include safes and ceiling fans; in the bathroom you'll find an extra phone, a hair dryer, and a terry robe. The great location offers quick access to the parks and to boating and water activities.

✪ **Disney's Yacht Club Resort.** 1700 Epcot Resorts Blvd. (off Buena Vista Dr.; P.O. Box 10000), Lake Buena Vista, FL 32830-1000. ☎ **407/934-7639** or 407/934-7000. Fax 407/924-3450. 642 units. A/C MINIBAR TV TEL. $269–$415 double; $395–$550 concierge-level double; $455–$1,385 suites. AE, MC, V. Free self- and valet parking.

This stunning resort features extensive sports and entertainment options in a turn-of-the-20th-century New England yacht club setting. Its Stormalong Bay—a big draw for families—is a huge free-form swimming pool and water park that sprawls over 3 acres and is shared with its sister property—the Beach Club. The nautical theme carries into nicely decorated rooms that sleep five and open onto porches or balconies. Amenities include ceiling fans, extra phones in the bathroom, and safes. Business travelers appreciate the concierge-level rooms on the fifth floor.

MODERATE

✪ **Disney's Caribbean Beach Resort.** 900 Cayman Way (off Buena Vista Dr.; P.O. Box 10000), Lake Buena Vista, FL 32830-1000. ☎ **407/934-7639** or 407/934-3400. Fax 407/934-3288. 2,112 units. A/C MINIBAR TV TEL. $124–$189 double. Children 16 and under stay free in parents' room. AE, MC, V. Free parking.

The Caribbean Beach offers good value for families. Set amidst 200 acres, the rooms are grouped in five Caribbean "villages" around a large duck-filled lake. The main swimming pool replicates a Spanish-style Caribbean fort, complete with water slide, kiddie pool, and whirlpool. There are other pools on the property and lakefront white-sand beaches in each village. A 1.4-mile promenade is a good place to jog or walk around the lake. Another bridge leads to Parrot Cay Island, where there are a short nature trail, an aviary of tropical birds, and a picnic area. The rooms are warming, with oak furnishings and two double beds with chintz bedspreads. In-room amenities include coffeemakers and ceiling fans; refrigerators are available for $6 per night.

✪ **Disney's Dixie Landings Resort.** 1251 Dixie Dr. (off Bonnet Creek Pkwy.; P.O. Box 10000), Lake Buena Vista, FL 32830-1000. ☎ **407/934-7639** or 407/934-6000. Fax 407/934-7777. 2,048 units. A/C TV TEL. $124–$189 for up to 4. AE, MC, V. Free parking.

Nestled on the banks of the "mighty Sassagoula River," this resort is a budget-minded stop offering child-oriented programs and facilities; adults traveling alone may prefer a more sedate setting. The mid-sized rooms are basic, yet they're decorated comfortably. You can choose among a stately colonial plantation, rural Cajun-style dwellings fronted by brick courtyards, or mansions on the Sassagoula River. Outside, you'll find Ol' Man Island, a woodsy 3½-acre recreation area, which has an immense swimming pool with waterfalls, a broken bridge, a water slide, a wading pool, and a playground. There are also a whirlpool and a fishin' hole, where you can rent poles and get bait to try your luck.

INEXPENSIVE

✪ **Disney's All-Star Movie Resort.** 1991 W. Buena Vista Dr., Lake Buena Vista, FL 32830-1000. ☎ **407/934-7639** or 407/939-7000. Fax 407/939-7111. 1,900 units. A/C TV TEL. $74–$104 double. Children 17 and under free in parents' room. AE, MC, V. Free parking.

This is the latest Disney budget property, a part of a 246-acre complex that includes the All-Star Sports and All-Star Music Resorts. Larger-than-life dalmatians leap from the balconies, and other huge Disney characters dot the landscape. Each of the All-Star resorts offers the "Bare Necessities," but they're the cheapest options within WDW. On the upside, Blizzard Beach is next door, which makes bathers happy in all but the coldest months. There's also a full-size pool. Visitors looking for quiet should look elsewhere.

ON U.S. 192/KISSIMMEE

This tin-glitz stretch of highway is dotted with fast-food eateries, burger barns, and T-shirt shops. Not what you'd call scenic, but it does contain inexpensive hotels and motels 1 to 8 miles from the Walt Disney World parks. Almost all provide or can arrange for shuttle service to the attractions. The cost usually runs $10 to $14 round-trip per person. To aid motorists, U.S. 192 has 30- to 40-foot mile markers for use as reference points.

MODERATE

Holiday Inn Nikki Bird Resort. 7300 Irlo Bronson Memorial Hwy., Kissimmee, FL 34747. ☎ **800/206-2747** or 407/396-7300. Fax 407/396-7555. 529 units. A/C TV TEL. $80–$119. AE, DC, DISC, MC, V. Free parking. Take I-4 to Exit 25B. It's 1.5 miles past the Disney entrance on left, between markers 5 and 6.

Here's another hotel with a roaming mascot. Nikki Bird, who strolls the grounds giving hugs, is just one of this property's family-friendly perks. There's a large game arcade in the lobby, and connecting rooms and rollaway beds are available. All rooms have a refrigerator, microwave, safe, and hair dryer. Children under 12 eat free at the full-breakfast buffet offered next door at Angel's Diner; nightly entertainment includes songs, puppet shows, and games. Free transportation is provided to WDW parks.

INEXPENSIVE

In addition to the accommodations described here, there are scores of other inexpensive, highly serviceable motels, including most major budget chains, within a few miles of the WDW parks.

Econo Lodge Maingate East. 4311 W. Irlo Bronson Memorial Hwy. (U.S. 192), Kissimmee, FL 34756. ☎ **800/356-6935** or 407/396-7100. www.enjoyfloridahotels.com. A/C TV TEL. $29.95–$109.95. AE, DC, DISC, MC, V. Free parking. From I-4, take Exit 25A; the motel is across the street from Medieval Times at marker 15.

This property is set well back from the highways, and it comes with bargain rates for those on a budget. A new lobby has been added to the hotel, which has good service and is kept clean. The hotel provides free shuttles to WDW parks, and transportation is available to other attractions. There's also a heated swimming pool.

Hampton Inn, Orlando Disney Maingate East. 3000 Maingate Lane, Kissimmee, FL 34747. ☎ **800/426-7866** or 407/396-6300. Fax 407/396-8989. www.hamptoninnmaingatewest.com. 118 units. A/C TV TEL. $79–$129 double. AE, DISC, MC, V. From I-4 take Exit 25B to U.S. 192 west for about 2 miles. Turn right on Maingate Lane.

Since this is one of the newer budget hotels in the Walt Disney World area, the rooms are modern and relatively unscarred. Expect cherry-wood furnishings with teal and burgundy appointments. The property is clean and nicely landscaped. Rooms are of average size, with connecting rooms and cribs available. This is a good place for large families or families traveling together. Other pluses are the free continental breakfasts, a pool, coin-operated laundry, a car-rental desk, free local calls, irons and ironing boards, coffeemakers, data ports, free in-room movie channel, 24-hour front desk, and free coffee and tea in the lobby 24 hours a day.

7   Where to Dine

Since you'll be spending the majority of your time in the Walt Disney World Area, it's important to know the following information regarding all restaurants sprinkled throughout the parks. Below is a very limited selection of WDW restaurants. A complete list of WDW restaurants is available online at **www.disneyworld. com**. For restaurants outside Disney, you can get online restaurant information at **www.orlandosentinel.com** and **www. go2orlando.com**. For more information on specific restaurants throughout Orlando, refer to *Frommer's Walt Disney World & Orlando.*

Almost every restaurant offers a children's menu and usually provides some kind of kids' activity (mazes, coloring, paper dolls) as well. The downside of restaurants that cater to children is that they are noisy. If that will ruin your appetite, remember this rule: The higher the prices, the fewer the children.

How To Arrange a Priority Seating at Walt Disney World Restaurants   Priority seating *isn't* a reservation. It means you get the next available table once you arrive. There may be a small wait, but if you don't use this system you'll be in for a longer one. To get priority seating at any WDW restaurant, call ☎ **407/ 939-3463.** You can book as far as 60 days in advance of your arrival. If you're staying in a Disney resort or official resort, you can also arrange priority seating at guest services or concierge desks.

At Epcot, you can also do it at the WorldKey interactive terminals at Guest Relations near Innoventions East, at WorldKey Information Service on the main concourse to the World Showcase, or at your restaurant of choice.

In the Magic Kingdom, you'll need to go to the restaurant.

In Disney MGM Studios, you can make arrangements at Hollywood Junction Station on Sunset Boulevard or at the restaurants.

VERY EXPENSIVE

✪ **Victoria & Albert's.** In Disney's Grand Floridian Beach Resort, 4401 Floridian Way. ☎ **407/939-3463.** Reservations required. Jackets required for men. Not recommended for children. Fixed-price meal $85 per person, $35 additional for wine pairing; $115 Chef's Table, $160 with wine. AE, MC, V. 2 dinner seatings daily, 5:45–6:30pm and 9–9:45pm. Chef's Table 6pm only. Free self- and validated valet parking. INTERNATIONAL.

It's not often that dining can be described as an event, but Victoria & Albert's, Disney's most elegant restaurant, deserves the distinction. Its intimate dining room is crowned by a domed, chapel-style ceiling; the exquisitely appointed tables are softly lit by Victorian lamps; and your servers (a maid and butler always named Victoria and Albert) provide deft and gracious service.

Dinner, a seven-course affair, is described in a personalized menu sealed with a gold wax insignia. The fare changes nightly. You might begin with an hors d'oeuvre of Beluga caviar with toast points or apple-smoked Colorado bison, followed by a Dungeness crab cake as a hot appetizer. Then, antelope consomme might precede a main course such as black bass with toasted couscous or a beef tenderloin with Cipollini onion risotto. English Stilton served with pine-nut bread, port wine, and a pear poached in burgundy, cognac, and cinnamon sugar sets up dessert, which might be vanilla bean crème brûlée or white chocolate and raspberry Chambord soufflé. There is, of course, an extensive wine list. Opt for the wine pairing, which provides an appropriate wine with each course and lets you sample a variety of selections from the restaurant's distinguished cellars.

MODERATE

✪ **Cape May Café.** At Disney's Beach Club Resort, 1800 Epcot Resorts Blvd. ☎ **407/939-3463.** Priority seating. Character breakfast $14.95 adults, $8.50 children; dinner $19.95 adults, $9.50 children 3–11. AE, MC, V. Daily 5:30–9:30pm. Free valet and self-parking. CLAMBAKE BUFFET.

A hearty 19th-century–style New England clambake is featured nightly. Sand sculptures and furled striped beach umbrellas create the ambience of an upscale seaside resort. Items on the buffet include New England chowder, steamed clams and mussels, corn on the cob, chicken, and red-skin potatoes cooked in a steamer pit. Other offerings include salads, barbecued pork ribs, smoked sausage, pastas, and a variety of fresh breads and desserts.

✪ **Rainforest Cafe.** Downtown Disney Marketplace; look for the smoking volcano. ☎ **407/827-8500.** Priority seating. Main courses $8–$20. AE, DISC, MC, V. Sun–Thurs 10:30am–11pm, Fri–Sat 10:30am–midnight. Free self-parking. CALIFORNIA.

Don't arrive starving. Waits of 2 hours are typical if you fail to call ahead for priority seating. Kids especially love the junglelike setting and call of the wild. This is one place where monkey business is encouraged. The food is pretty good, too. Try unusual delicacies like Rasta Pasta—bowtie noodles mixed with spinach, roasted red peppers, broccoli, and Parmesan cheese smothered in a garlic-pesto cream sauce. Top off your meal with the excellent coconut bread pudding with dried apricots. There's a good selection of beer and wine. The tables are very close together, so those with physical disabilities may find it difficult to maneuver here.

MEALS WITH DISNEY CHARACTERS

Especially for the 10-and-under set, it's a thrill to dine in a restaurant where costumed Disney characters show up to greet the customers, sign autographs, and pose for family photos. Make reservations as far in advance as possible for these very popular meals.

The prices for these character meals are pretty much the same no matter where you're dining. **Breakfast** (almost all serve it) is usually $14 to $16 for adults and $8 to $10 for children; those that serve **dinners** (we've noted them below) are $19 to $22 for adults, $9 to $13 for children 3 to 11. Prices vary a bit, though, from location to location.

To make **reservations** for any WDW character meal, call ☎ **407/939-3463.** American Express, MasterCard, and Visa are accepted at all character meals.

Artist Point. 901 Timberline Dr. (at Disney's Wilderness Lodge). Daily 7:30–11:30am.

In a rustic lodgelike dining room with a beamed ceiling supported by tree-trunk beams and large windows providing scenic lake views, Pooh, Tigger, and other critters from the Hundred-Acre Woods host an all-you-can-eat buffet breakfast.

Garden Grill. In The Land Pavilion at Epcot. Daily 8:30am–8:10pm.

This revolving restaurant has comfortable semicircular booths. As you dine, your table travels past desert, prairie, farmland, and rain-forest environments. Hearty family-style meals are hosted by **Mickey, Minnie,** and **Chip 'n' Dale.** American breakfast and lunch choices are extensive. Dinners include several entrees (roast chicken, farm-raised fish, and hickory-smoked steak), mashed potatoes, vegetables, biscuits, salad, beverage, and dessert.

✪ **Liberty Tree Tavern.** In Liberty Square in the Magic Kingdom. Daily 4pm–park closing.

This colonial-styled 18th-century pub offers character dinners hosted by **Mickey, Goofy, Pluto, Chip 'n' Dale,** and **Tigger** (some or all of them). Meals, served family-style, consist of salad, roast chicken, marinated flank steak, trail sausages, mashed potatoes, rice pilaf, vegetables, and a dessert of warm apple crisp with vanilla ice cream. Food-wise, this is the best character meal in the World.

Index

See also Accommodations and Restaurant indexes, below.

FROMMER'S® COMPLETE TRAVEL GUIDES

Alaska
Amsterdam
Arizona
Atlanta
Australia
Austria
Bahamas
Barcelona, Madrid &
 Seville
Beijing
Belgium, Holland &
 Luxembourg
Bermuda
Boston
British Columbia & the
 Canadian Rockies
Budapest & the Best of
 Hungary
California
Canada
Cancún, Cozumel &
 the Yucatán
Cape Cod, Nantucket &
 Martha's Vineyard
Caribbean
Caribbean Cruises & Ports
 of Call
Caribbean Ports of Call
Carolinas & Georgia
Chicago
China
Colorado
Costa Rica
Denmark
Denver, Boulder & Colorado
 Springs
England
Europe

European Cruises & Ports
 of Call
Florida
France
Germany
Greece
Greek Islands
Hawaii
Hong Kong
Honolulu, Waikiki &
 Oahu
Ireland
Israel
Italy
Jamaica
Japan
Las Vegas
London
Los Angeles
Maryland & Delaware
Maui
Mexico
Miami & the Keys
Montana & Wyoming
Montréal & Québec City
Munich & the Bavarian
 Alps
Nashville & Memphis
Nepal
New England
New Mexico
New Orleans
New York City
New Zealand
Nova Scotia, New Brunswick
 & Prince Edward Island
Oregon
Paris

Philadelphia & the
 Amish Country
Portugal
Prague & the Best of the
 Czech Republic
Provence & the Riviera
Puerto Rico
Rome
San Antonio & Austin
San Diego
San Francisco
Santa Fe, Taos & Albuquerque
Scandinavia
Scotland
Seattle & Portland
Singapore & Malaysia
South Africa
Southeast Asia
South Pacific
Spain
Sweden
Switzerland
Thailand
Tokyo
Toronto
Tuscany & Umbria
USA
Utah
Vancouver & Victoria
Vermont, New Hampshire
 & Maine
Vienna & the Danube Valley
Virgin Islands
Virginia
Walt Disney World &
 Orlando
Washington, D.C.
Washington State

FROMMER'S® DOLLAR-A-DAY GUIDES

Australia from $50 a Day
California from $60 a Day
Caribbean from $70 a Day
England from $70 a Day
Europe from $60 a Day

Florida from $60 a Day
Hawaii from $70 a Day
Ireland from $60 a Day
Italy from $70 a Day
London from $85 a Day

New York from $80 a Day
Paris from $85 a Day
San Francisco from $60 a Day
Washington, D.C.,
 from $60 a Day

FROMMER'S® PORTABLE GUIDES

Acapulco, Ixtapa &
 Zihuatanejo
Alaska Cruises & Ports of Call
Bahamas
Baja & Los Cabos
Berlin
California Wine Country
Charleston & Savannah
Chicago

Dublin
Hawaii: The Big Island
Las Vegas
London
Maine Coast
Maui
New Orleans
New York City
Paris

Puerto Vallarta, Manzanillo
 & Guadalajara
San Diego
San Francisco
Sydney
Tampa & St. Petersburg
Venice
Washington, D.C.

FROMMER'S® NATIONAL PARK GUIDES

Family Vacations in the
National Parks
Grand Canyon

National Parks of the
American West
Rocky Mountain

Yellowstone & Grand Teton
Yosemite & Sequoia/
Kings Canyon
Zion & Bryce Canyon

FROMMER'S® MEMORABLE WALKS

Chicago
London

New York
Paris

San Francisco
Washington, D.C.

FROMMER'S® GREAT OUTDOOR GUIDES

New England
Northern California

Southern California & Baja
Southern New England

Washington & Oregon

FROMMER'S® BORN TO SHOP GUIDES

Born to Shop: China
Born to Shop: France

Born to Shop: Italy
Born to Shop: London

Born to Shop: New York
Born to Shop: Paris

FROMMER'S® IRREVERENT GUIDES

Amsterdam
Boston
Chicago
Las Vegas

London
Los Angeles
Manhattan
New Orleans

Paris
San Francisco
Seattle & Portland
Vancouver

Walt Disney World
Washington, D.C.

FROMMER'S® BEST-LOVED DRIVING TOURS

America
Britain
California

Florida
France
Germany

Ireland
Italy
New England

Scotland
Spain
Western Europe

THE UNOFFICIAL GUIDES®

Bed & Breakfasts in
California
Bed & Breakfasts in
New England
Bed & Breakfasts in
the Northwest
Beyond Disney
Branson, Missouri
California with Kids
Chicago

Cruises
Disneyland
Florida with Kids
Golf Vacations in the
Eastern U.S.
The Great Smoky &
Blue Ridge
Mountains
Inside Disney

Hawaii
Las Vegas
London
Miami & the Keys
Mini Las Vegas
Mini-Mickey
New Orleans
New York City
Paris

Safaris
San Francisco
Skiing in the West
Walt Disney World
Walt Disney World
for Grown-ups
Walt Disney World
for Kids
Washington, D.C.

SPECIAL-INTEREST TITLES

Frommer's Britain's Best Bed & Breakfasts and
Country Inns
Frommer's Britain's Best Bike Rides
The Civil War Trust's Official Guide
to the Civil War Discovery Trail
Frommer's Caribbean Hideaways
Frommer's Food Lover's Companion to France
Frommer's Food Lover's Companion to Italy
Frommer's Gay & Lesbian Europe
Frommer's Exploring America by RV
Hanging Out in Europe
Israel Past & Present

Mad Monks' Guide to California
Mad Monks' Guide to New York City
Frommer's The Moon
Frommer's New York City with Kids
The New York Times' Unforgettable
Weekends
Places Rated Almanac
Retirement Places Rated
Frommer's Road Atlas Britain
Frommer's Road Atlas Europe
Frommer's Washington, D.C., with Kids
Frommer's What the Airlines Never Tell You